The Career-Minded Student

The Career-Minded Student

Neil O'Donnell

*This book is dedicated to my nieces and nephews:
Anne, Katie, Casey, Erin, Max and Ryan. I am so very
proud of all of you and know you will all make the
world a better place.*

*Love,
Uncle Neil*

Contents

1	Introduction	1
2	Time Management	19
3	Fundamental Study Habits for Success	33
4	Advanced Study Habits for Success	49
5	Selecting and Researching a Major	60
6	Exploring a Major and Gaining Experience	68
7	Getting the Most out of Internships and Early Jobs	74
8	Tech-wise	83
9	Your First Job Search	87
10	Interviewing Skills	94
11	Concluding Remarks	112

Chapter 1

Introduction

College and high school students have it tough. They are told that they need a college degree to achieve success, and then they are told what few degrees the "experts" consider to be of true value. Finally, these weary students are sent off with little training on how to succeed academically and to prepare to compete for jobs right after graduating with a college degree and little to no relevant experience. No wonder why college students are so stressed and too often fail to graduate. This book is meant to compensate for this failing of American educational systems.

With twenty plus years providing academic, career and personal counseling to college students, I have compiled a list of steps for students to take to excel in their college classes, to gain useful career insight and to be competitive for jobs immediately after graduation. From experience, students who follow these steps usually excel in their classes, graduate with a degree and obtain a job in their chosen field soon after graduation. Having read too many reports about the low graduation rates at colleges and universities, and having heard countless students rightfully complain of the lack of realistic preparation they are given, I wrote this book so that students besides my own advisees would have a blueprint for success. Now, before diving into the pages of advice herein, there are a few things I think you should be aware of.

First of all, I don't care what degree you pursue. It's your life and you should follow the path that best fits your abilities and interests. I obtained both a bachelor's and a master's in Anthropology and am quite happy with the career I've had. It's funny, quite a few people told me Anthropology was a "useless" degree. Yet, my studies in Anthropology well prepared me for all my jobs, and I am more than satisfied with my subsequent career. To that end, I will not tell anyone what degree or career path to pursue. It's your decision just as Anthropology was mine. What is important is that you research yourself and your career interests to see what major best fits your career and personal goals. Don't worry, we'll cover degree and career research later on in this book.

A second thing to recognize is that a bachelor's or graduate degree (master's or doctorate) are not necessary for every career path. However, 'higher education' is necessary whether that education is an associate's degree program at an accredited community college or a trade school (carpentry, plumbing, etc.). In some instances, an online certificate program may be all that you need to get started on your career path. Whatever the case, gaining knowledge beyond high school is generally required. That is why it is critical that individuals study their career interests as soon and as thoroughly as possible to determine the level of higher education needed.

Lastly, you will notice I provide a lot of study strategies in this book. Why? Career success is often dependent on doing well in classes, because you won't get a college degree if you don't pass your classes or do well in a job if you failed to retain relevant knowledge and skills. Consequently, it is imperative to enter college with the skill sets needed to excel academically. Otherwise, all your career preparation will be useless as most good paying jobs require a college degree in order for a job applicant to even be considered for an interview.

Special Note to Transfer Students

Transfer students have long been a concern for colleges and universities as this pool of students generally struggles to find academic and, ultimately, career success. From my discussions with transfer students, I found that they often feel lost in or ignored by their new college or university. At the same time, I found that transfer students were unfamiliar with all the resources their new campus had and were reluctant to seek help. A major reason for my writing this book was in fact to confront this dilemma. We, the faculty and staff of colleges and universities, want our transfer students to be as successful as every other student on the campus. We want transfer students to ask us for academic and career guidance. You truly matter to us; just ask for help whenever needed. For starters, I recommend that all transfer students find a mentor/advisor within her/his major department and meet with that mentor bi-weekly. This should be done within the first month after admission to the college. Also, transfer students should attend any orientation programs offered by their new college. These programs will help familiarize students with the campus layout and academic resources, not to mention faculty students will likely take classes with at some point. Remember, these programs offer a great opportunity for students to get questions answered.

Next, a transfer student should visit the college's career center and familiarize herself/himself with the center's resources connected to the student's major. Lastly, transfer students should join a club connected with their major or one of their hobbies. From my experience, transfer students who follow through on this advice tend to achieve academic and career success.

Getting Started

As with any journey or quest, it's important that readers make some preparations before setting off. For college-bound students, undergraduate or graduate, I have listed here some pearls of wisdom, things which I wish I had been more understanding of as I began my college journey.

- **This is your journey and yours alone!** Parents, teachers, friends and others will provide all sorts of advice on what majors and career paths you should pursue. They are well intentioned, but much of the advice given is based on hunches. When I was in high school, guidance counselors and other educators pushed students towards a small set of careers, most emphasis placed on biology, chemistry and computer science. I actually intended on pursuing biology with a focus on marine studies, but anthropology and the study of other cultures dominated my interests during my first semester. Thankfully, my parents pushed me to pursue my interests. I am quite happy with my major and career choice twenty years after graduating from college, and I owe a lot of that to having pursued my interests. Meanwhile, I watched a lot of friends and students, pushed by family and teachers, struggle through STEM majors (Science, Technology, Engineering and Mathematics) until they either switched majors or dropped out of college. Why did many of these students struggle? As a tutor and academic mentor, I found a lot of students struggling with STEM classes because they were not truly interested in the material. They actually were more interested in Communications, English, History or something else, but they bowed to outside pressure. As for the actual job market, things rarely work out the way "experts" anticipate. I know quite a few STEM graduates who took a long time to find employment after graduation where as my friends with Arts and Humanities degrees **often** found degree-related (and good paying) employment right after graduation, if not before. What really made the difference for most? Those interested in their studies seemed more energized about their field and likewise entered the job market enthusiastically.

- **It's going to be tough at times!** A college is not going to just give you a degree, nor do you want them to. As with all parts of life, you will face struggles while in college and investigating/pursuing career options. Accept that! When you encounter such struggles, reach out to professors, tutors, counselors, friends and family to help you through. We all need help at times, and you should never hesitate to ask for it. As an FYI – I am a certified stress management coach and spend considerable time every week teaching students ways to confront, manage and mediate stress. The last chapter of this book contains a listing of strategies to help readers deal with their stress. For now, I just want to emphasize that most every college or university has staff like me who are trained and skilled at teaching stress management strategies for students. Make use of these services.

- **Go equipped!** A hiking enthusiast, I never venture into the wilderness without basic supplies; to do so would be hazardous to my health and well being. The same can be said of students venturing into the world of higher education. Consequently, students should enter college their first day with essential supplies which includes:

- *A large plastic tote for providing a watertight container for those documents a student should keep until after graduation.* Specifically, students should preserve the syllabus from every course they take as well as textbooks, dittos or other handouts related to a student's major or long-term career goals. Yes, I am in favor of students holding onto some textbooks, particularly those relevant to their major and career goals. Why? It is difficult to retain all crucial information presented in a college class, at least long-term. Having an undergraduate textbook as a reference could prove of vital importance later on in graduate school or on the job when suddenly a student needs to gain quick access to information and the internet is down. I've been there; trust me.

- *A collegiate dictionary (and actually look up words you are unfamiliar with otherwise the dictionary is useless).* There is a lot of jargon that is major/career-specific, which makes this dictionary especially important to have when taking classes within your intended major. For definitions not in the dictionary, ask the professor for an explanation and thorough definition.

- *A notepad that you keep with you at all times (use this pad for writing down names, addresses, words you need to look up later, etc.).* Keep this with you at all times, and replace it when you run out of blank pages. What did I use my pad for? Ideas for research paper topics (as well as thesis statements for papers – such ideas always seem to spring up at weird times), the titles of books a professor recommended, and the names of people I was told could provide me with needed information. As a final suggestion, keep the pad near your bed along with a penlight so that if you think of a great idea at night you will be more likely to write the idea down and thereby retain it. How often do people really remember an idea the next morning? For those who say "I have an app on my phone for writing notes," what happens if your battery runs out or a liquid gets on your phone or laptop? *Paper notepads need no batteries.*

- *A professional email address that you check daily (an email account with a username that is not cutesy or vulgar such as 'yourname@email.com' instead of 'iamawesome@email.com' or 'sexy3000@email.com'*). If you are dead-set on an email that bears an unusual or potentially inappropriate username, set up the more 'professional' email so that it forwards all messages to your preferred email. Why? First of all, emails with unusual or 'inappropriate' usernames will often be filtered into an individual's Junk Mail folder. Secondly, professors and/or employers will often see inappropriate email usernames as a sign of immaturity and a lack of professionalism. Not the impression a student wants to make to someone with the potential to provide a job or a letter of recommendation. Hiring managers, in particular, often will not take a job applicant seriously if her/his application was sent via email and the email username was deemed 'inappropriate'. Many great applicants have been overlooked or straight out rejected for a lack of a professional email (fair or not).

- **An emergency fund (the larger the better, but at least $50).** A warning for all undergraduates: emergency expenses WILL arise. It's inevitable! You should have cash readily available to deal with such emergencies. For a start, a cash reserve of $50 will provide for basic necessities in an emergency: food, clothing, or cab fare. Yet, as a student takes on more responsibilities and acquires more possessions (a car for example), those emergencies become bigger and costlier. Even the smallest and quite routine car repairs alone cost upwards of $100. I will let others argue the finer points of cash versus a bank account. Yet, I will add one final point. Don't take on any expenses that aren't essential. In particular, don't purchase or lease a car until it is absolutely necessary, especially since many colleges now provide students with free or discounted yearly passes to public transportation to students. Even if your car is trouble free throughout a given year, you are still looking at a approximately $200 in yearly oil changes, fifty dollars in a yearly inspection and a couple thousand dollars in fuel. For the record, rarely are car repairs not going to pop up especially if you purchase a used vehicle.

- ***Basic 'office' supplies to include a stapler, a hole puncher, 2 to 3 refillable mechanical pencils/lead, 3 to 5 pens, paperclips, a roll of quarters, and a roll of duct tape (plus a backpack or duffle bag to carry the supplies in).*** These are supplies that will be of use throughout your college years and well into your career as well. As such, it's worth it to spend a little extra and get quality items, particularly when purchasing a stapler and a hole puncher (and make certain you pay extra for a device that punches three holes in paper at once as the single hole puncher makes it more difficult to make even punches). As for pens, just make certain you have a few readily accessible at all times (blue or black ink, whichever you prefer). As for pencils, I recommend students splurge a bit and buy mechanical pencils, because mechanical pencils don't need to be sharpened during an exam or in class while taking notes. If mechanical pencils are not an option, make certain to buy a pencil sharpener, a small one that collects and holds pencil shavings. For paper clips, a box of 100 will likely last a couple years if not throughout an undergraduate career. A roll of quarters ($20 worth) will provide for emergency expenses such as a phone call (when a cell phone is dead and a public phone is the only alternative) or a late night snack from a vending machine when staying up to study, write a paper, or read a book. As for the duct tape, such a universal tool can seal a torn backpack, provide an emergency patch to a coat or bind plastic sheeting to cover a broken car or dorm window. Having spent my life in Buffalo, duct tape has diverted snow, water and ice in all those situations, at least for me.

- ***Two flash drives or portable hard drives (save digital copies of all your syllabi, papers and other assignments until you graduate).*** Use one of the drives as a backup in case the other fails, and store it in a secure, dry location. Password-protect both hard drives as well. If you don't know how to password-protect a drive, ask your college's computing staff for assistance. Additionally, you should change passwords routinely (a minimum of once every 3-6 months) to better protect your files. FYI – the flash drives often given to freshmen during their college orientation program that bear the college's logo are generally cheaply made and fail often within the first month of use. It is worth it to spend money of a dependable brand name. My personal preference for flash drives is Kingston followed by Imation, Memorex, Lexar, SanDisk and PNY. Flash drives are also known as memory sticks, thumb drives and jump drives. Please stop saying 'jump drives'. Please. Jump drives are what power the Battlestar Galactica and should only be used to refer to 'faster-than-light' engines. Just sayin'.

- ***One folder per class each semester.*** Folders are cheap ways to get organized right from the semester's start providing a safe location for a course syllabus as well as any other printouts provided by the course professor. Still as low as $.25 in many discount stores, I recommend students buy new folders every semester. If your finances permit, purchasing plastic folders that can be inserted into a binder is a good, durable option also. To reduce the risk of taking the wrong folder to class, pick a different color folder for each class.

- ***Printouts of current guidelines for Modern Language Association (MLA) and American Psychological Association (APA) citation styles, which can be obtained online for free (you need to learn these guidelines as soon as possible and can gain assistance through professors, teachers and tutors).***

Students, when writing papers, need to properly cite where they obtained their information. Failure to do so can result in a charge of plagiarism, a hefty charge that could lead to a student being expelled from a college. Most professors require the use of either the MLA or APA citation styles so have the guidelines on hand right from the start of your first semester. Take the time to learn these styles as soon as possible (tutors and English professors are often the best resources to speak to when learning to properly cite in a paper).

- **Be prepared and accept your responsibility to ask questions!** As you interact with professors, college staff and professionals in various fields, you are going to hear unfamiliar industry terms and the names of people you don't know. Ask for clarity on anything or anyone you are unfamiliar with. Your retention of information and ultimate success depend on this. For students uncomfortable raising their hand and speaking up in class, ask your questions after class or during a professor's office hours. The professor won't know students didn't understand something unless a student asks a question so YOU need to speak up. For the record, any question you have is likely a question several others in the class have. The difference? You had the courage to ask the question.

- **Find time to have fun!** Remember my comment that it would be tough at times? Prepare for that inevitability. Take time to read a novel, go to a movie with friends, join a club related to your career or personal interests, visit family on weekends, participate in a monthly/bi-weekly book club, or go hiking. Such activities will help reduce stress levels of even the busiest undergraduate. However, waiting until stress hits a high level will reduce the effectiveness of these stress relievers. Consequently, I recommend you pick one or two activities and make each a part of a weekly routine. Personally, I read every night before bed and hike every weekend, habits I picked up in college which continue to provide relief from even the most difficult of days.

Habits for Success

Before getting into specific advice for college students or any job seekers, I wanted to impart some wisdom that benefited me in life, particularly with regards to my career. Not surprisingly, the wisdom was passed onto me from my parents, both of whom were hard-working, industrious individuals determined to succeed. While neither of my parents could afford to attend college, they both continually read and sought out other opportunities to educate themselves including attending lectures at local colleges and work seminars. All in all, my parents' actions and words helped me and my siblings recognize personal habits that would increase the likelihood of our own career success. These traits include:

- **Get and continue getting educated!** My parents required us to attend at least one year of college or some other higher education program (trade school, certificate program, etc.). They recognized that not everyone needs a college education to succeed, but Mom and Dad wanted to further instill the idea in us that education is an ongoing process; there is no end to it. If you want success, you must continually seek to expand your knowledge-base by reading history, keeping up on current events, or exploring your chosen field beyond classroom lectures either through volunteering, shadowing a professional, or an apprenticeship. A good day is a day in which you learn at least one new thing. For the record, more than twenty years after graduating with my Bachelor of Arts in Anthropology, I still am continuing my education recently earning certifications in Career Coaching, Integrative Mental Health, Stress Management, and Tutor Training. The path of education never ends.

- **Plan for contingencies!** Few things completely work out as planned: extra guests show up for an event, emergency expenditures popup during a vacation, and a surprise snowstorm occurs in early October to thwart long-planned outdoor gatherings. Now, it is doubtful any amount of planning can prepare for everything, but my parents certainly tried to anticipate problems ahead of time as much as possible. To all readers, I recommend that you try to maintain an emergency fund, have a friend or relative you can stay with should your apartment lose power, and have a backup transportation plan in place for getting to and from classes/work *before* it's needed, because cars breakdown and public transportation shuts down periodically. Basically, prepare for things to go wrong *before* they go wrong. No, all problems cannot be anticipated. Yet, preparing for contingencies related to important events or activities can only help you.

- **Be on time!** Being late was never an option for my siblings and me. Whether it was for school, dinner or bed, we had to be on time. To this day, I am always early for work just as I was always early for class. Did I mention I only missed one class as an undergraduate student? Why the importance of being early? Does it really make a difference? In class, being five minutes late could cause a student to miss critical information needed for an upcoming exam. At work, tardiness could result in loss of a promotion or the job itself. As for a job interview, being late could nix a person's chances of *ever* getting a job at the company doing the interviewing. Being late has a way of impacting an individual's education and leaving a lasting, negative impression with others, ultimately making it difficult for a person to achieve success.

- **Say thank you!** My parents always made a point of sending thank you notes to anyone who helped them. First of all, saying thank you is the right thing to do whenever someone assists you. Secondly, a simple thank reflects a good character, something friends, colleagues and potential employers will remember. Think about it. Who would you rather work with? The person who takes you for granted or the person who shows gratitude towards others? Down the road, when in a job years out of college, showing good character could help land an individual a promotion or a new job.

- **Learn from mistakes!** My parents are not perfect, and they would be the first to admit that. Yet, my parents rarely make the same mistake twice. Accept that you will make mistakes in the future: in school, work and life. When a mistake occurs, consider how you should have handled the given situation, make a mental or written note of the resolution, and move on. Trust me, professors and employers alike understand mistakes, but neither are particularly forgiving of repeat offenses.

- **Forgive!** Someone somewhere at sometime or another is going to hurt you or your reputation. Often times, such events are accidental or even imagined. Regardless, as my parents taught me, learn from the experience, make every effort to mend fences, and forgive. Admittedly, you may wish to be cautious around the guilty party in the future. Yet, holding tightly to anger usually does nothing more than cause you to suffer and struggle to move forward. Let it go! If you find difficulty in moving past such a situation, seek support from a trusted colleague or even a counselor.

Chapter 2

Time Management

A pivotal part of the guidance herein is dependent on readers obtaining a higher education. This is not to say that everyone needs a bachelor's degree, or any college degree for that matter, but education in your chosen field is necessary for career success. In the fields of carpentry, plumbing and culinary arts, an apprenticeship with a master could provide sufficient education with which to attain knowledge and jobs. Also, many colleges now offer 'certificate' programs that suffice for enough education to attain employment in certain fields. Regardless of the path chosen, a job seeker will need to attain an education. How does one succeed in higher education? The first step revolves around time management.

Time Management

There are only 24 hours in a day for a total of 168 hours in a week. Sound like a lot? That number is probably smaller than you realize. Let's check. For an exercise, estimate the amount of time you spend on the following activities (If easier to tally hours per week for any of the above, calculate hours per week and divide by 7):

Figure 1

Eating	_______ Hours/Day
Sleeping	_______ Hours/Day
Getting dressed/washed	_______ Hours/Day
In classes	_______ Hours/Day
Studying	_______ Hours/Day
Interacting with Family and Friends	_______ Hours/Day
Watching TV	_______ Hours/Day
Doing chores/working	_______ Hours/Day
Checking email	_______ Hours/Day
Utilizing Social Media	_______ Hours/Day
	_______ Total Hours

You can find printable version from here: https://www.dropbox.com/s/64eb007crzmw48c/figure1.pdf?dl=0

Now, total up the amount of hours spent on these activities per day and then multiple that number by

7. Is the total number equal or greater than 168? If the number is less than 168, congratulations, because you have that much remaining time to spend as you wish. If the number is greater than 168, as often happens when students complete this type of exercise, don't worry. It simply means you are not as clear in your use of time as you should be, which is something you can and should work on.

Time management is a critical skill for those looking to succeed. Talk to friends and family members whom you consider successful, and ask them how they spend their days. More often than not, you will find successful people can account for almost every minute of every single day, including weekends. Successful individuals tend to keep regular hours for sleeping and eating and often set aside time for everything from household chores to reading a book or watching television. This does not mean successful individuals never vary from a written schedule. However, adherence to a schedule tends to keep an individual focused, determined and on time. Additionally, for success, it is necessary to adjust a time management plan when needed. Why? Emergencies and surprises happen particularly during classes and/or work. Without using any semblance of a time management plan, adjusting for such contingencies becomes a much greater exercise. Now, before getting to emergency adjustments, let's start with a basic time management plan. First of all, it's best to have some sort of planner in which to write down class times, work hours, study times and assignment due dates. Admittedly, daily planners can be a bit expensive. However, a lot of discount stores like 'Dollar Stores' sell planners for just a couple of dollars. Another alternative is to generate a weekly planner with Windows Word, Excel or a similar program, print out fifty-two copies, add respective dates, and store them in a one inch binder.

Figure 2: Sample Planner Page

March 1-7	Monday 3/1	Tuesday 3/2	Wednesday 3/3	Thursday 3/4	Friday 3/5	Saturday 3/6	Sunday 3/7
7-8am							
8-9am							
9-10am							
10-11am							
11am-12pm							
12-1pm							
1-2pm							
2-3pm							
3-4pm							
4-5pm							
5-6pm							
6-7pm							
7-8pm							
8-9pm							
9-10pm							
10-11pm							

You can find printable version from here: https://www.dropbox.com/s/vrihqn9oxgmjltu/figure2.pdf?dl=0

Now for the second step: actually use the planner. I received a planner during my college orientation program. I never used it. As a result, my time management skills were hampered quite a bit my freshman year: I missed due dates for assignments, failed to remember of extra credit lectures I could have attended, and forgot about tests until last minute, which severely limited my time to prepare. Planners are only effective if we utilize them, plain and simple.

For those new to time management, I always recommend starting off small to develop the habit of planning each day. Begin with the following:

- **List time for meals!** I find that having a set meal time for dinners and lunches makes it easier to stick with my time management plan. College students, due to their varying class and work schedules, will have difficulty with having one set time for lunch and dinner, but some regularity should be possible to maintain. As a side note, make certain you actually take time each day to eat breakfast, lunch and dinner. These meals help keep students energized during classes. Without that energy supply, it will be hard to focus in class and impair a student's ability to understand and retain information.

- **List times for sleeping!** I purposely left off 11pm to 7am on the sample chart, because this is time that should be spent sleeping. Experts suggest a minimum of anywhere from 8 to 10 hours of sleep for optimum health and cognitive functioning. Yet, as a realist, I know college students think they just need a couple hours to get through the day. I urge my students to get at least 6 to 8 hours and to be in bed before midnight. I also recommend students maintain the same sleep hours every day of the week, including Saturday and Sunday. That consistency, during college and later career years, will help individuals with maintaining an overall time management plan. For the record, I personally find that when I don't maintain a consistent sleep or meal schedule, my stress increases while my ability to combat stress lessens.

- **List class, lab and work times!** Your daily planner should also include the times each day that will be spent in classes and/or at work. For classes, write down the room the class meets in or if it is an online class. If working multiple jobs, write down the specific job worked each day. *Full time students should limit work hours as student grades and retention of course material tends to suffer when working more than fifteen hours per week.*

Figure 3

March 1-7	Monday 3/1	Tuesday 3/2	Wednesday 3/3	Thursday 3/4	Friday 3/5	Saturday 3/6	Sunday 3/7
7-8am	Breakfast	Breakfast	Breakfast	Breakfast	Breakfast	Breakfast	Breakfast
8-9am							
9-10am	Math	Work Study	Math	Work Study	Math	Work/Store	
10-11am		Work Study		Work Study		Work/Store	
11am-12pm	Spanish	Work Study	Spanish	Work Study	Spanish	Work/Store	
12-1pm	Lunch	Work Study	Lunch	Work Study	Lunch	Work/Store	Lunch
1-2pm	Biology	Work Study	Biology	Work Study	Biology	Work/Store	
2-3pm						Work/Store	
3-4pm							
4-5pm		Dinner					
5-6pm	Dinner	History	Dinner	Dinner	Dinner	Dinner	Dinner
6-7pm		History		Anthropology			
7-8pm		History		Anthropology			
8-9pm				Anthropology			
9-10pm							
10-11pm							

You can find printable version from here: https://www.dropbox.com/s/f97et85358733uq/ figure3.pdf?dl=0

This basic format provides a great start for undergraduate students as well as graduates entering the workplace. After practicing for a couple weeks, start adding more day to day details to further organize each day. For example, add times for continuous activities such as going to the gym, a monthly book club, a weekly gathering with friends at the movies, or even a weekly television show you cannot miss. Additionally, students should include due dates for assignments and the dates of tests and quizzes along with set study times throughout the week. The following example incorporates all the aforementioned advice.

Figure 4

March 1-7	Monday 3/1	Tuesday 3/2	Wednesday 3/3	Thursday 3/4	Friday 3/5	Saturday 3/6	Sunday 3/7
7-8am	Breakfast	Breakfast	Breakfast	Breakfast	Breakfast	Breakfast	Breakfast
8-9am	Study	Study	Study	Study	Study		
9-10am	Math	Work Study	Math	Work Study	Math/Exam	Work/Store	
10-11am		Work Study		Work Study		Work/Store	Study
11am-12pm	Spanish	Work Study	Spanish	Work Study	Spanish	Work/Store	Study
12-1pm	Lunch	Work Study	Lunch	Work Study	Lunch	Work/Store	Lunch
1-2pm	Biology	Work Study	Biology	Work Study	Biology	Work/Store	Study
2-3pm	Gym		Gym		Gym	Work/Store	Study
3-4pm	Study	Study	Study	Study	Study	Study	
4-5pm		Dinner				Study	
5-6pm	Dinner	History	Dinner	Dinner	Dinner	Dinner	Dinner
6-7pm	Study	History	Study	Anthropology	Study	Study	
7-8pm	Study	History	Study	Anthropology	Study	Movies	
8-9pm		TV - NCIS		Anthropology	TV – Big Bang Theory	Movies	
9-10pm		Study				Movies	
10-11pm				ANT Paper due by Midnight			

You can find printable version from here: https://www.dropbox.com/s/z2p8a0pxdqc7jf7/figure4.pdf?dl=0

Notice that not every hour is accounted for. From my experience, you cannot account for everything so having some open free time helps in addressing emergencies: car repairs, meetings with professors, overtime at work. Likewise, I find that I still have days where I need to rearrange my day last minute because of unforeseen circumstances or forgotten meetings. Accept that everyone will encounter such days.

Again, from experience, I find that those with a plan/schedule in place find it easier to adjust to emergencies. I also know that I personally continually worked on my time management skills until I had a system in place. How did I practice time management and enhance my skills in that regard? I found, early on in my undergraduate career, that some professors changed assignment due dates continuously. Consequently, I always seemed to be adjusting my scheduled time for studies and home work. To make things easier, I used the upper right-hand corner of the first page of notes (for each class each day) to write down a reminder of my plans for the rest of the day. If surprises popped up, I would make adjustments as needed. I would review these impromptu schedules at the end of the class day at around 4pm to finalize my schedule for the evening. This addition to my time management plan served as a great way to better evaluate my time and responsibilities and undoubtedly helped me excel in my time management and classes.

Figure 5

○		3pm to 4pm – ANT study group fireside lounge 4pm to 5pm – library research for HIS paper 5pm to 6pm – Dinner in Student Union 6pm to 7pm – Read Anthropology Ch. 7 8pm to 9pm – Watch NCIS 9pm to 10pm – Review notes from Day's Classes

You can find printable version from here: https://www.dropbox.com/s/6o5efb0nqt6plcg/ figure5.pdf?dl=0

Today, more than twenty years removed from my undergraduate years, time management remains a major concern for me as well as a reason for my successes. As readers transition from college to the work place, here are a few additional strategies to consider, which may just help them succeed as well.

- **At the end of each day, write down a list of tasks you need to complete the following day and leave it on your desk. Then, in the morning, review the list and check off tasks as you complete them.** This seemingly simple idea can significantly increase an individual's productivity by simply refreshing a person's mind. Think about it. Taking time to write a list and then reading it over in the morning helps our memory. You see? Simple. For the record, the last thing I do at work each night is write a list of tasks I need to complete the next day, and the first thing I do every morning is to look over that list and adjust my daily schedule to make room for the completion of those tasks. This action absolutely

energizes me. What's more, this list helps reduce my stress level, because I have a plan of
attack for the day instead of feeling frustrating
having to come up with a daily schedule each
morning.

- **Whether you decide to use a com-
puter/phone based planner or a traditional paper planner, make certain to
check it daily to refresh your memory
of upcoming task deadlines and events.**
This may sound a bit redundant, but there
is a difference between a daily task list and
your overall calendar. The overall calendar
has routine events scheduled, events that you
might overlook if you fixate on the daily list
of prioritized tasks. Reading over your daily
schedule daily will lessen the likelihood of
missing a long standing meeting. This planner
is something that you should check EVERY
day, even Saturdays and Sundays. With smart
phones, tablets and internet cafes all around,
there is no reason a student or professional
cannot access that planner. As probably the
last person in the United States without a cell
phone, I was able to still find internet access in
some extremely remote areas of the country.
So, there is no reason for not checking that
planner daily. Failing to check an planner
could lead to missing out on a chance for a
great job or promotion. Worse, failure to check
a planner daily might lead to an individual
being fired.

- **Maintain a primary email account for business/career-related activities. Check that email daily and adjust your plans/calendar immediately should you receive a message indicating event changes (time and/or date of event).** Email is the preferred mode of communication for growing majority of people today. As such, it is crucial to keep tabs on any email that involves potential changes to your schedule. As an undergraduate, a change in a meeting with a professor for tutoring could make it difficult to do well on the next test. As a professional, missing an email with a schedule change for a meeting with the CEO, a meeting you subsequently miss, could lead to a loss of your job.

- **Maintain a calendar/planner backup, because computers, phones and even old fashioned paper planners get lost, damaged or stolen quite often. At the very least, have major events and relevant details recorded on two separate planners/calendars.** Regardless of what format you keep a calendar (digital or paper), I strongly advise everyone to keep a backup calendar. Paper calendars get wet or shredded, online calendars get corrupted, and excel spreadsheet-based calendars get deleted. Picture, if you will, spending hours putting in due dates for papers or later on in life listing countless appointments with your supervisors when in the workforce. Then, BAM! You lose your daily planner or the phone you stored information on. Reboot data from the Cloud, you say? BAM! You files stored on the Cloud are eradicated by a virus, and you only learn of that after you lost your smart phone. Yes, this may be an unlikely occurrence, but it highlights a reality that comes up now and then. Therefore, it is imperative that major events, due dates and personal dates of great importance (i.e. birthdays) be recorded on a second calendar. The great rule of thumb is to have two paper calendars for important dates and then spend one day in December, in the days before New Year's, and transfer the important dates to new calendars for the coming year. Sound like overkill? Trust me that you will be thanking me should anything happen to one of these calendars.

- **Put vacation time in every calendar!** Breaks from work AND college are vital for individuals to relax and to reinvigorate drive, determinations and one's commitment to educational, career and personal goals. Unfortunately, way too many students and professionals don't make real vacation time a priority, which leads many to burnout. Burnout, in turn, leads to many college students failing to finish college and many professionals to losing their edge in the workplace. By incorporating vacation time into a schedule, a student or professional increases the likelihood of her or his taking that vacation. Why is this so important? Stress, fatigue and self-doubt increase when an individual is not taking time to relax, and all three of those commodities will make it difficult for even the most determined student or professional to achieve success.

- **Change schedules carefully!** Changes to anyone's schedule is inevitable. Just accept that truth. There is no way to predict college, work or personal emergencies that will necessitate the canceling of a meeting or the need to miss a class or tutoring session. So, when emergencies arise and schedule changes are necessary, thoroughly examine your schedule to find an appropriate time to reschedule a missed event for. At the very least, look over the next two weeks in a schedule to see the ramifications of schedule changes. Will the new event time or location impact other events? Additionally, if you miss a class for any reason, obtain medical or other documentation supporting the importance of your absenteeism. This is a critical thing because an absence in a class may lead to a lower final grade. This is good practice anyway, because professionals often have to submit medical documentation when missing a work event. Of course, for a professional, lack of appropriate documentation could lead to loss of pay or loss of a job.

- **Review your schedule continually!** College students and professionals often have a lot going on, which makes it difficult to remember every appointment, class or meeting an individual needs to attend. Consider the schedule example from earlier in the chapter; how easy would it truly be to remember all of that? I think it is a good policy for everyone to review the day's and week's schedule in the morning and during lunch every day. Doing so will lessen the likelihood of failing to prepare for scheduled events in addition to lessening the chance of missing an event altogether.

- **Be early!** Many professors start classes exactly on time while many professionals begin meetings exactly on time. Makes sense doesn't it? Consequently, doesn't it seem odd that so many people show up late for class and/or meetings? Honestly, everyone is late now and then, but for many, tardiness is a habit. Being late for a class could hurt a person's grade as he or she may miss vital notes for an upcoming test. Meanwhile, being late for a job interview or a critical business meeting in the professional realm could lead to a loss of a job. Developing the habit of effectively managing time will help most in avoiding being late and thereby having either an educational or a professional career put in jeopardy.

Chapter 3

Fundamental Study Habits for Success

Regardless of the career path pursued, an individual will likely need to continue her or his education beyond high school. For some, being an apprentice to a tradesman or gaining a certificate in any number of fields (medical coding, legal assistant, personal trainer), will be sufficient to ensure entry into a successful and fulfilling career. Many career paths today require a Bachelor's or even a graduate degree just to attain entry-level positions. That said, whether you are going for a certificate or you are planning to get a Master's degree, you will need higher education. Consequently, as part of my advisement for readers (and all my students), I include a dose of study skills guidance with my career advice, because studying, learning and achieving academic success is critical to an individual's ultimate career success. Anyone who fails to devote significant time and focus to her/his studies will have limited career options. With graduate degrees in higher demand, it's often necessary to have a college GPA of 3.0 or higher as an undergraduate, which makes academic success even more vital for college students planning a career. Furthermore, with technologies, methods and theories changing over time in most fields, continuing education trainings are now often required of even senior-level employees. To those ends, the following study techniques are a foundation which can lead students to academic and, ultimately, career success.

Class Essentials

Let's start with the basics, which are, unfortunately, too often ignored by students. First, if you want to succeed in a class you need to attend class regularly. As an undergraduate student, I missed three classes (not three days), and I actually showed up for two of those classes, but was sent home because I was so sick. Essentially, I missed/skipped one class in my nine semesters as an undergraduate. *I dare you to beat that!*

Now, I admittedly showed up a number of times when I legitimately should have stayed home and worked on getting well. Yet, aside from one inexcusable absence, I attended classes regularly, which allowed me to hear lectures, take notes, participate in class discussions, and take surprise quizzes. When skipping a class, a student misses information often vital to her/his career and personal growth. A student also loses out on an opportunity to get questions answered, questions about lecture material, proper career methodology, or what an upcoming test will cover. Students must treat their undergraduate studies as a full time job, which it essentially is. Instead of receiving a pay check, students receive guidance and information that will help them advance in their ultimate career. If you want to succeed in a job and get a paycheck or promotion you have to show up. Likewise, any student wishing to excel in classes and ultimately attain knowledge and a degree must attend classes. As for the classes where the professor doesn't take attendance? Don't be fooled. Many professors don't want to "baby sit" students and prefer to spend more time lecturing rather than taking attendance. These professors expect students to be responsible and know information covered regardless of why any given student missed/skipped a class. Consider yourself warned.

What do you do in the event of an absence? Be responsible and inform the professor why you missed the class and ask what material was covered. Also ask the professor and fellow students if you could read over their notes from the lecture. Lastly, don't make a habit out of skipping class.

In conjunction with class attendance, students need to purchase and carry required materials for class including textbooks, paper, pens and pencils, and any other materials the professor indicates. Without necessary materials/equipment, the student is essentially skipping class (see above) and will likely not gain valuable information needed for tests or later on for her/his career.

Lastly, at least with regards to class essentials, students need to obtain, read and keep hold of the class syllabus. This is essentially a contract between students and their professors. The syllabus should be provided by the professor on the first day of class and detail what is expected of the student (number of tests, required text books, details regarding research papers, etc.). Reflecting back on time management, students should record any due dates listed on a syllabus into their planner. I also recommend that students hang onto syllabi beyond their graduation and through graduate school, particularly classes related to the students' major(s). Why? Some graduate schools may request details of undergraduate classes in determining whether or not a student needs to complete additional course work. I was able to have both statistics and foreign language requirements waived because of undergraduate coursework I completed.

Note Taking

Showing up to class is not enough. Students must be active learners to get the most out of the classes they are attending. Would you pay to see a movie and then sit throughout the movie with you eyes closed and ears covered? I didn't think so. As you can imagine, active learning includes recording information provided by your professors, which usually equates to note taking. Now, after years being a student and a professor, I've seen students sit through class without writing one piece of information down. True, there are times that a professor rambles on without providing any new information, but those instances are few and far between. As for the students not taking notes, they are usually the students that fail or do poorly in the class. Likewise, these are the students that usually struggle to find professors willing to advise or write letters of recommendation for them.

What should you record in your notes? Aside from instances where a professor clearly indicates a student should or should not worry about a lecture topic, it can be difficult to determine what information is worth recording in a notebook. The following strategies will help students isolate important information from the extraneous data:

- Write down definitions and any examples the professor uses to illustrate a word's meaning.

- Write down the names of important individuals discussed and a list of their achievements.

- Write down anything the professor discusses in detail and/or explores in detail through PowerPoint slides or drawings on either a chalk or smart board.

- Write down events a professor discusses at length or anything the professor discusses with a change in intonation or volume.

As professors tend to cover enormous amounts of information each class, students need to fine-tune their note taking skills to increase their writing speed and provide space for notes a professor may add to a previously discussed topic. As for increasing writing speed, I advise students to develop a collegiate short-hand: symbols to replace commonly used words such as in the following cases:

Figure 6

Symbol	In Place Of
>	Greater Than
<	Less Than
&	AND
#	Number
=	Equals/Equal To
≠	Does Not Equal/Not Equal To
+	Plus/Add/And

You can find printable version from here:
https://www.dropbox.com/s/z8586aj6gcdd8um/
figure6.pdf?dl=0

With regards to managing notes and reserving space for future comments or illustrations, the "Cornell" note taking system is one to consider. Named for the institution of its origin, the Cornell note taking system provides a great way for students to manage notes during lectures and later for study and summary purposes. In this system, students are advised to draw two lines on their notebook paper; one line is drawn to separate approximately the bottom fifth of the page while a second line is drawn down the length of the notebook paper separate one third of the page. As indicated in the provided example, the largest section of the notebook paper is set aside for notes taken during class.

The second section, adjacent to the 'Notes' section, provides space for students to write down key terms or questions related to the respective notes. This section is a space also where a student can add supplement information the professor provides at a later date or an indication that the professor suggested that particular section of notes will likely be on the upcoming test. The final section, near the bottom of the page, provides space for students to summarize the notes written in the other two sections.

Figure 7

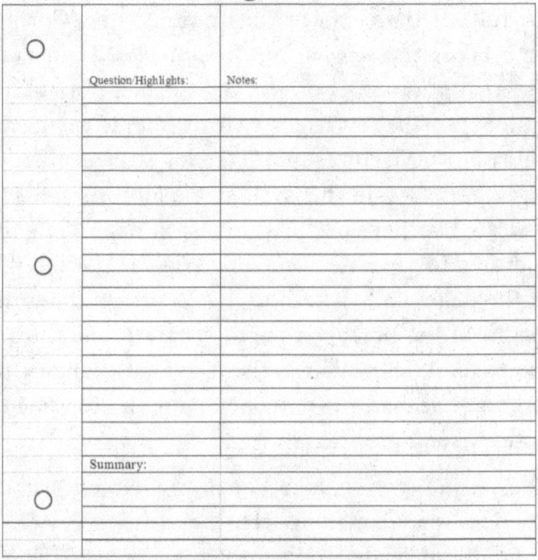

You can find printable version from here:
https://www.dropbox.com/s/r3fzldf6217j2fo/
figure7.pdf?dl=0

Now, it is not enough for a student to take thorough and accurate notes. Students also must review the notes taken in class and not just once or twice. There are multiple interpretations of the amount of time students need to spend reviewing notes, and resulting time estimates hinge, usually, on the total hours per week a student should review notes. I prefer to highlight the critical times when students must study notes. First, immediately after a class ends, it's important for a student to go somewhere quiet to review the notes just taken in class. If a student has another class immediately after then he/she should wait for the first available break. During a time period of twenty to thirty minutes, students should review the notes and write down a list of questions they have regarding the lecture material. Additionally, this time allows an opportunity for students to rewrite words or names that are barely legible as recalling/interpreting what the words or names are will only get tougher with each passing day. Later that same day (between 7pm to 10pm), review the notes from that day's class once more for twenty to thirty minutes. If a student has three classes in a given day, that equates to three evening study sessions (twenty to thirty minutes per class). Again, students should look for any material that does not make sense and write down questions they have. Bring any questions to the professor's attention immediately either during office hours or the next class.

This foundation of studying will take students a long ways towards comprehending and memorizing class material. This is not to say that this is the only studying required for student success; students should continue to review notes throughout each week and on weekends as well. However, studying twice in the first twenty-four hours is crucial as to delay review of notes even a few days will hamper a student's ability to comprehend and recall material later on.

As an aside, it is during the evening study sessions when I used to create flash cards for terms, people or events, especially those mentioned in both class lectures and textbook reading. I realize that many students consider flash cards to be a child's study aid, but in reality, flash cards are effective tools for all age groups and aid in the reviewing and recalling of information. For visual learners who feel flash cards are too wordy for their needs, draw pictures in place of words to illustrate important information. In the end, students should adjust any and all aids to fit their specific needs and preferences.

Class Participation

We already covered the issue of attendance, but I feel obligated to add an addendum to the previous discussion. Sitting in a chair in the lecture hall is not enough. Students MUST participate in class as well. What does that mean? It means class is not a time period for checking email, Facebook or Twitter, let alone making/answering phone calls. Students not engaged in the discussion, whether through listening or speaking, are simply a distraction for the professor and the other students. Do you really want to spend hundreds or thousands of dollars per class to just sit and stare at walls? What's more, do you realize a professor can remove you from a class (in other words fail you) if you are not participating? Being a distraction aside, not actively participating in class discussions will lessen the likelihood a student will comprehend or retain material covered, which will ultimately make it difficult for a student to pass a class, let alone get an A. Asking questions, offering input, and engaging the professor and other students in debates is a way to overcome class boredom and better understand and retain information. Additionally, as many professors take class participation into consideration when compiling a student's grades, actively participating can help a student achieve a higher final grade.

As for the asking of questions to gain clarification of subject matter, I know it can be embarrassing to raise your hand and speak in front of classmates. What if I look stupid for asking a question that everyone else already knows? What if the professor thinks I am not taking the class seriously? These are the same questions I dealt with, and I can assure you asking questions is not something to be embarrassed about. First of all, it takes courage to ask questions; students and professors realize this. Secondly, the question a student asks is often the same question many other students have but are too frightened to ask. Thirdly, we professors want students to ask questions; we see questions as a sign that students are trying hard to truly understand the material. For professors, a student asking a question shows us the students are interested in the material and are taking the discussion seriously. In a nutshell, asking questions is important. For those who struggle to ask questions and speak in class, see the professor before or after class if not during office hours to ask questions and get the answers you need.

One last remark regarding class participation is something students and professors should pay heed to: be respectful of others contributing. As one of millions battling an anxiety disorder, it took a great deal of effort for me to speak up in class. I worked hard over time to get to the point where I could give an oral report. I started by writing down questions to ask before class began and forced myself to ask more and more questions until I was an 'active' participant. It was particularly difficult to get comfortable speaking in class when I watched a student shout out over others and shut down fellow classmates. Not only is this rude, it's also a behavior that makes it difficult for everyone to learn. Most issues discussed in class leave room for alternate, supportable opinions. Not allowing someone to voice an opinion may ruin everyone's chance to better understand the topic at hand. In college, such behavior could lead to failing or expulsion. In the career world, such behavior could lead to loss of significant revenue, contracts and, ultimately, a job.

Reading

Often times, tests and quizzes in college courses are based entirely on assigned textbook readings. Yet, as important as textbook readings are, many students never read a textbook after buying it. Is it any wonder such students struggle to achieve academic success?

Accept that it is a student's responsibility to read textbook chapters to better understand class lectures and to prepare. This doesn't mean skimming textbook chapters a few days before a test. Instead, students need to read chapters thoroughly over a period of time if they are to truly benefit from and retain information covered. Now, I am well aware that textbooks are not the most riveting reads. Nevertheless, students cannot ignore textbooks and rely just on class notes. How does a student manage all this, reading all textbook chapters and fighting off boredom? First, learn to start reading early and break up reading times into manageable sections. Set up times throughout the week for reading textbook chapters and plan things out so that you can read a given chapter over the course of several days and still finish all reading before the next class exam. What did I do in college that worked well? I would read for twenty to thirty minutes and then take a ten minute break during which time I would drink water or eat a light snack. Be careful during this break. If you turn on the television or glance at email and/or Facebook, you will likely then get caught up in that and never return to the assigned reading.

After the ten minute break, I would return to the textbook chapter and continue reading. Again, after twenty to thirty minutes, I would take a ten minute break. In total I would read a textbook chapter for two to three periods after which I would move on to something else. Why? I found that anymore time spent on one textbook would make it hard to stay focused and motivated.

In addition to reading, students should take notes of important topics, persons or events discussed in the text, what many refer to as "outlining" the chapter. Outlining in this context involves writing down textbook chapter headings and the providing a summary of information in a given textbook section. It is often recommended that students consider chapter headings as questions to be answered by the text that follows, a technique designed to help students glean the most from text. Take the following text as an example and observe the "outline" that follows.

Dr. A.L. Benedict

A highly skilled medical doctor by trade, Dr. A. L. Benedict was also an archaeologist in Buffalo, New York during the start of the Twentieth century. Using the city's system of trolley cars, Benedict traveled throughout the region discovering sites and collecting artifacts, mostly from prehistoric Iroquoian sites. With excavations focused on prehistoric Native American sites, Dr. Benedict became a recognized expert on Iroquoian society and archaeological investigations and research. In 1901, Dr. Benedict's accomplishments warranted his assignment as the superintendent of the Ethnology Building at the Pan-American Exposition where he assembled one of the greatest displays of prehistoric societies ever assembled

Outline of Reading:

1. **Dr. A. L. Benedict (Who was Dr. A.L. Benedict)**

   - **Medical doctor and archaeologist**

   - **From Buffalo, NY; worked on Iroquoian and prehistoric sites**

   - **Superintendent of the Ethnology Building at Pan-American Exposition**

This example shows a basic outline. The length and detail of an outline's content will vary based on the textbook content and a student's attention to detail, but greater familiarity with this process with help a student refine outline entries considerably. Ultimately, after compiling outlines for textbook chapters, students end up with literal study guides, which could be useful aides for future class quizzes and exams. To further enhance these outlines, students should compare these outlines with class notes. Any material that appears in both is likely to show up on exams. Additionally, these outlines become an effective way to review textbook chapters without having to reread the textbook.

Regarding reading strategies, let's end with a caution. Many students waste time with highlighting textbook pages, because they end up highlighting entire pages. Since the goal of highlighting is to isolate important tidbits of information for later reference, how is highlighting entire pages helpful? I found it more helpful to add notes in pencil in the margins of textbook chapters denoting important information.

Chapter 4

Advanced Study Habits for Success

Attending class, taking notes, reading textbooks and *retaining* information will take students only so far. Students must be able to *process* the information they learn to attain a true education as well as to earn good grades on assessments including research papers and tests. Likewise, students must develop a learning routine for college success and to prepare for lifelong learning.

Papers

English 101 and 102 are the basic writing requirements for college students. With the occasional requirement of remedial writing classes and/or the addition or one or two "writing intensive" courses, that is the bulk of writing training students receive within higher education. Consequently, students receive little opportunity to expand their writing skills, which is why professionals across all fields lack strong writing abilities. Sure, colleges and universities offer tutoring services to help students just as many professors put in long office hours to assist students, but where is the incentive? How do we convince students of the importance of using English 101 and 102 (or their equivalents) to the fullest? I've got an idea?

To students reading this book, let me fill you in on a little secret. Those of us with strong writing skills have more career options and more advancement opportunities than our competition. Given the rise in digital media use as well as the growing need for grant writing in public and private sectors, businesses, non-profit and for-profit alike, are increasingly dependent on the generation of articulate, concise and moving copy for advertisements, press releases and other assorted writings. Even email correspondence is highly scrutinized by administrators, many of whom have important emails proofed by strong writers on their staff. Do I have your attention now? Look at English 101 and 102 as opportunities rather than requirements, and get every college paper proofread by a tutor or a professor before submitting. Do this, and you will be well on your way to becoming a standout writer in an ever-growing pool of job applicants.

Now, as for rules for writing, I've heard quite a few, and often times, what works for one professor is grounds for failure for another. That said, I want to impart wisdom I gleaned from writing multiple fiction and non-fiction books and from editing countless manuscripts for students and colleagues. First, keep your introductory paragraphs short and to the point. When introductions get over five sentences (for a college paper mind you), I find the writer often fails in articulating a main thesis and maintaining order throughout the paper. I also find in these instances that the writer is herself/himself failing to understand the true thesis and related data. Papers are great tools as they can guide us in processing information for ourselves as well as our readers. Read your introductions critically and ask yourself if it's truly clear and to the point you are trying to make. Frankly, I still spend most of my time on introductions given their importance. Once you are satisfied your introduction is clear, have a tutor or professor proofread it. Let someone else verify its clarity. There is no room for egos here as even the most accomplished writers usually have others proofread their writing. For those who say "I will write the intro after I finish the paper," you're just making things more difficult. The introduction, if clear and concise, will help you maintain order and focus throughout the entire paper. Spending quality time on the introduction from the beginning will make the paper writing process more bearable. It will also aid you in better processing the information that is detailed in the paper.

While we're discussing introductions, let's tackle another major rule I follow, which corresponds to the thesis statement. A paper's thesis statement is critical to keeping a writer and reader focused. After generating a thesis, writers should ask themselves if the thesis matches the assignment. Likewise, does the thesis clearly list the major issues and arguments to be covered? Again, I think it's important for students to have professors or tutors evaluate their introduction and thesis statement early on to prevent going off topic. If any inconsistencies exist, make changes before moving on to the body paragraphs. Believe me, I know the frustrations of working out a clear thesis statement and the desire to just go onto the body of the paper thinking, "I'll just fix things later." The real problem is that your struggles with creating a plausible thesis likely mean you need to reread and gain a better understanding of the relevant research. Remember, you are in the process of learning the material you are writing about so it's okay if you struggle with the material. Just ask your professor for help; we professors want you to.

Moving on to the body paragraphs of a paper, writers cannot just randomly provide evidence. Rather, the order of evidence should reflect how the evidence was presented in the thesis statement. A thesis statement is not just to introduce the paper's topic, it should also provide details of the points to be argued and the order such points will be presented in. For an example, take a look at the following thesis statement.

"Katniss Everdeen's greatest strengths were her devotion to family, her devotion to justice and her hunting skills."

This sample thesis statement, referencing the lead character from Suzanne Collins' Hunger Games Trilogy, clearly shows the paper's theme/topic [Katniss Everdeen's greatest strengths] as well as the writer's chosen points [devotion to family, devotion to justice and hunting skills]. If a reader, after seeing that thesis, read the first body paragraph and found it to be a discussion of Katniss Everdeen's hunting skills, he/she would likely be a bit confused having expected Everdeen's 'devotion to family' to be the first point presented. While a reader will likely be able to work things out for most basic college papers, you never want a reader to get confused. Taken a step further, if your professor sees such a discrepancy, your grade on a paper will suffer.

Moving onto the conclusion, the last paragraph is as critical as all previous ones. First, the conclusion should provide a brief recap of the paper's thesis and arguments. If a writer starts talking about J.R.R. Tolkien's character Gandalf in the conclusion when the previous paragraphs and thesis revolved around Suzanne Collins' character Katniss Everdeen, a reader is going to get confused. Stay on topic in the conclusion or, again, your grade will suffer.

In a final note about writing papers, let's tackle the issue of citations or, more to the point, plagiarism. Any solid paper will be supported by evidence, information gleaned from books and/or articles to support a writer's argument. Writer's cannot just "borrow" information from such sources. Instead, credit must be given by 'citing' where a statement or quote came from. After more than twenty years of working in higher education, I have found most instances of plagiarism are due to a writer not properly citing (as opposed to the outright and deliberate theft of another's writings). This in mind, I urge all students and writers to take time to learn how to properly cite information. For assistance, seek aid from librarians, tutors and professors. It will be time well invested.

Test Prep

There is no greater assessment of a student's understanding and retention of class material than a test. Likewise, there is no greater stressor of students, but such stress is avoidable. How? It all comes down to preparation. Test anxiety and poor test performance are all avoidable if a student spends sufficient time preparing for tests early. Again… how? I'm glad you asked.

Building from the aforementioned study and reading strategies, it's important to start test preparation immediately after the first class. The first tools I recommend all students use are flash cards. Many college students baulk at such study aids, because they consider flash cards to be a child's study device. Such critics couldn't be further from the truth and are only denying themselves access to a study technique proven effective for all age groups. Of course, there are other college students who complain that flash cards "don't work for them." In over twenty years of tutoring, I've yet to come across a college student for whom this was true, especially after meeting with a student to discuss flash card formats. Give flash cards an honest chance, and you'll be glad you did.

As for flash card designs, it's best to keep things simple: a word, historic event or person's name on one side and relevant information on the reverse. For you visual learners, use drawings or other images in place of names or information. There is no law dictating how a student has to design a flash card, so it's best to design the cards to fit the students learning style. Once you create a flash card, get in the habit of looking each one over periodically until the connected assessment (test or quiz). The key here is to continually study the cards. Otherwise, the cards are of little educational value.

The next tool in a student's test preparation arsenal is a study guide. Often given out by professors, study guides are incredibly helpful is preparing for tests. My recommendation is that students use study guides to focus on related topics in notes, in readings and on flash cards. The key here? Students should not wait to review and use a study guide. What if the professor doesn't give out study guides? Make your own, and for increasing the subsequent study guide's effectiveness, ask the class professor to look it over and give feedback. Any assistance from the professor in this regard can aid the student further.

After flash cards and study guides, I advise my students to generate their own sample test questions. Essentially, I ask students to put themselves in the role of the professor and develop sample quizzes or tests to study from. How? Take information from textbook readings and class notes to generate multiple choice, true/false and/or essay questions. For example, look back to the sample reading on Dr. A.L. Benedict we discussed earlier. For a basic sample question, a student could ask herself/himself the following:

- Who was Dr. A.L. Benedict?

Frankly, I think more specific questions help students more. For instance, a student should, in this instance, consider creating sample questions such as:

- How did Dr. A.L. Benedict travel to sites in order to excavate?

- What building at the Pan-American Exposition did Dr. A.L. Benedict work at and in what capacity?

- How successful was Dr. A.L. Benedict in his assembling and displaying of Native American artifacts?

A critical key with generating sample questions is to do so early and often. For a start, create three to five questions for every lecture and/or chapter reading. How effective is this test prep strategy? Generally, I find students do significantly better than their peers on tests when they employ this technique. Try it out. You'll be amazed how often the sample questions you make resemble, almost word for word, the questions that end up on the actual test.

A final test prep strategy I'd like to discuss is the infamous 'study group'. Why 'infamous'? Study groups can be effective, but they can also be very damaging to a student's learning and preparation for tests. If everyone in the study group is failing, how helpful can a study group actually be? Consequently, for students looking to study groups for help, keep the following in mind to ensure a study group is a help rather than a hindrance:

- Everyone in the study group must be expected to contribute, which includes attending class and keeping up on assigned readings.

- Study groups should be started as early in the semester as possible.

- Add students to the group who are doing well in the course if possible.

- Ask the professor or a tutor to join the group weekly.

- Test each other with flash cards and sample test questions periodically.

Collectively, these are the test prep strategies that have been most helpful to me and my now countless students. As for those who battle test anxiety (myself included), I find that those students who enter a test prepared are less likely to be impacted by severe test anxiety during a test (getting a good night sleep and nutritious breakfast beforehand help as well). For those students whom suffer from an anxiety disorder (myself included), it is essential to seek assistance from a college's counseling center in addition to utilizing the aforementioned strategies. There is no shame in seeking out such help. In fact, it's a brave thing to do and something I regret not doing earlier.

Continuing Education

So, what happens after you graduate? Before you cheer about no more papers or tests, you need to remember that the world is forever-changing. No industry is immune to this reality so it behooves everyone to update their skills regardless of the field they are in. I for one attend monthly continuing education workshops online and at conferences to hone my counseling, tutoring and advisement skills. Doing so helps me keep abreast of new theories and methods to help me and my clients/students as it also helps me acquire continuing education credits needed to maintain my certifications. Additionally, something young graduates should especially keep in mind, conferences and similar venues offer a chance to network. As we will cover in later chapters, networking is a great way to find employment particularly when the economy is struggling. Yet, whether it's for knowledge or networking, continuing your education after graduation is a must. Otherwise, you're going to fall behind your competition and find yourself unemployed and worse, unemployable.

Chapter 5

Selecting and Researching a Major

With the requisite 'effective study skills' discussion done, it's time to turn to one of the book's and every college student's primary concerns: what major or career should a student pursue? Now, there are certainly enough books, articles and "experts" touting their own view. However, most of these opinions are coming from sources with limited experience in higher education, academic advisement, career guidance and making dramatic career changes themselves. What about me?

From early on in life, I loved sharks, creative writing and the study of foreign cultures. These loves continue on to this day. As college drew near, my goal was to become a marine biologist and study great white sharks. Now, in high school, I struggled with science classes, both academically and interest-wise. Meanwhile, I excelled in social studies and ancient history subject matter. I ended up taking an anthropology course my first semester and was hooked, particularly with the idea of archaeology, a subfield within anthropology. Anthropology, the comprehensive study of Humanity, truly proved to be what contented me, and my parents supported my decision. Meanwhile, countless others suggested I not pursue anthropology since I would "never find a job." Fortunately, I didn't listen to these naysayers.

I gained field experience in archaeology and cultural anthropology, my primary specializations, and even found paid anthropology-related positions during summers before graduating. I continued working in my roles as a field archaeologist and as an academic support specialist (a position my cultural anthropology expertise aided) after graduation until I soon landed a grant-funded position at a museum where I served as the curator of the Native American collection. I continued to serve as an academic and career advisor for undergraduates throughout my years at the museum, work which only increased my interest in advisement and working with a diverse population. After the grant finished, I quickly found a full time position at a private college where I served as an academic support specialist and career advisor. I continue to work in this capacity today though I now work at my alma mater. As for my love of sharks and creative writing, I help advocate for the protection of sharks and write novels in my spare time; I found a way to pursue all my interests. Why the quick biography here? I wanted to show readers my path towards a career as I find my struggles and successes are not so unique.

Many students go into college with one career path in mind and then end up changing their major three to four times. From there, many college graduates go off in a new direction completely after graduating and need a master's degree as their undergraduate degree doesn't match well with the new career pursuit. I wrote this book to help students avoid this trap. Why did I have such success with a degree many consider of no value? It ultimately came down to the fact that I selected a major that fit my interests and my skills rather than a major that others perceived would lead to financial success. This is the very advice I want to advocate here.

Selecting a Major

Your chosen major and career is just that: yours. Consequently, you should be pursuing things that interest you. How's that for insightful? College students should consider and investigate their options and interests as soon as possible, which means the first semester they attend college. How does a student start investigating her/his interests? Whether a student is totally undecided or committed to a major, her/his first step should be to take a career assessment like the Strong Interest Inventory or the Myers-Briggs Type Indicator. Such assessments, usually available through a college's career center, are not tests that will indicate the profession a student was born to pursue and excel in. Rather, these assessments will match a student's responses to a series of questions about her/his interests to relevant majors and careers. After completing the assessment, students should then make an appointment with the assessment's administrator (usually counselors at the career center). This is a vital step that many students skip. Why is this step so important? While students can undoubtedly glean useful information from an assessment on their own, career center counselors are trained to provide comprehensive interpretations of career assessments for students so that students get the most out of the assessment.

Career Assessments

- ✓ Strong Interest Inventory
- ✓ Myers-Briggs (MBTI)
- ✓ FOCUS

Additionally, career center staff can immediately direct students to reading materials, web sites and professors best suited to provide more information about respective majors. In preparation for that meeting, a student should do and bring the following:

- Write a list of jobs/careers he or she is interested in.

- Write down a list of five and ten year career goals.

- Write down a list of future personal accomplishments (own a house, be married, have traveled, etc.).

Once a student has identified prospective majors from a career assessment or through other means, he/she needs to do some detailed research. This doesn't mean just doing a Google search on a career path or major. It means spending hours researching job opportunities and responsibilities, regions where such majors are in need, and whether or not graduate school is necessary for jobs within a major/career path. Specifically, students should:

- Check their college career center for publications regarding a major or career.

- Check the career center and other campus offices to see if any lectures or presentations are scheduled, which cover majors/careers of interest to the student.

- Ask relevant departments for brochures related to career options.

- Speak with relevant professors about their experiences in the field and what range of jobs might be an option for majors.

Now, this research is just a beginning, mind you. In addition to these basics, students must actually follow up all information this research uncovers. If there is a lecture about a major or career a student is interested in, he/she needs to actually attend the workshop to obtain the information. As for speaking with professors about majors and career paths, follow through on advice a professor gives. If a professor recommends that a student speak to another professor or a professional off campus relevant to the major, the student must follow through and contact the respective professor/professional. When meeting with professors or professionals within a major/career, ask:

- What level of education is needed to get a job?

- What is the range of jobs accessible with a given major?

- What courses in other majors would better prepare one for the field?

- What internships and/or volunteer experiences would provide the best background for going into the field?

- What part time or full time jobs, open to undergraduates, would provide the best insight into a major/career as well as be good experience to have on a résumé?

The last question is of particular importance and one not many students ask as freshmen or sophomores. Frankly, relatively few people encourage students to think about such a question that early in an undergraduate's college career, but it is something to take to heart as soon as possible. Why? Getting experience in a major early on will help a student determine if he/she chose a suitable career path, better in many cases than any coursework. Additionally, experience gained, preferably beginning the summer after freshmen year, will help a student build up relevant experience with which to better compete for jobs immediately after graduation. Likewise, this experience could help a student create a network of contacts who will be helpful for locating and obtaining jobs after graduation.

Once an undergraduate finds one or two potential majors to pursue, he/she should take introductory coursework in the relevant major(s). Remember, introduction courses can be a bit overwhelming as they usually cover a large range of topics although in just brief detail. Don't let a difficult introductory class dishearten you. Instead, seek out assistance from professors or tutors to better understand and retain information. If after taking an introductory and/or upper level class a student decides the major is not a good fit, he/she needs to go through the aforementioned steps again. This may seem overwhelming, but it is better to spend time early on doing the research as opposed to getting a degree and then realizing an entirely different major would better suit a student's interests and goals. In instances where a student obtains a Bachelor's and then decides to pursue a new career, a Master's degree could serve as a bridge to the new field. A graduate school may require the student in such instances to complete relevant undergraduate courses before acceptance into a Master's program. However, usually a student will not have to obtain a second Bachelor's/major.

Chapter 6

Exploring a Major and Gaining Experience

While we visited the importance of exploring a major in the previous chapter, I thought it useful to walk readers through the process with a little more clarity through examples. In my personal experience, I wasted little time in exploring anthropology, my ultimate major and career path. Starting with my first freshman semester, taking Introduction to Cultural Anthropology with Dr. Simeon Chilungu, I asked about what the field entailed, what career options I would have and how to gain experience. Through Dr. Chilungu, I learned of the diversity of markets and environments anthropologists could work in including healthcare, criminal justice, education and multiple public venues. For me, being a field archaeologist and working as a tutor/academic advisor were my greatest interests. Consequently, Dr. Chilungu and my academic advisor, Dr. Roslyn Berkovitz, advised me to speak with campus professionals with experience in field archaeology and tutoring/academic advisement. I got right to work.

Beginning with the tutoring and academic advisement side of things, I volunteered at the Educational Opportunity Program's tutoring center, specifically working first in the computer lab. While not paid for my time, I learned a great deal about office management, customer service and computer programming, all of which are skills I've used in every job since. While volunteering at the center, I also had the opportunity to watch tutors and academic advisors work with students. By the end of my first college semester, I was well versed in the academic advisement of students and even served as a supplemental advisor for many undergraduates. Additionally, having utilized tutors while working in the center, I gained familiarity with and a love of tutoring and mentoring. This work truly meshed with my interests, and for experience, I continued volunteering at the center until I was hired as the anthropology and a writing tutor my junior year. My exploration of archaeology followed a similar trajectory.

I signed up for an Introduction to Archaeology and Physical Anthropology course my second semester to learn more about the field. Early on in the semester I asked the professor, Dr. Donald Mitchell, about career options and opportunities for archaeologists. While experienced in archaeological fieldwork, the professor advised me to speak with the department's chief archaeologist, Dr. Engelbrecht. It's important here to note Dr. Mitchell's advisement as a professor you speak with may not be the best source of information. In such cases, ask professors who else on campus could provide guidance. Why? Professors are likely to know their colleagues' specialties and be able to send you to the best advisors early on, which will ultimately save you time (thanks Dr. Mitchell).

Taking Dr. Mitchell's advice, I met with Dr. Engelbrecht and asked endless questions of the man who would become my department advisor (thank you for your patience and guidance Dr. E). The major questions I asked included:

- What courses should I take within anthropology and other majors to best prepare myself for graduate school and employment in archaeology?

- What is the range of jobs that an anthropologist/archaeologist can attain?

- What archaeologists in the community would be good to speak with about other career options/experience?

- What field experience could I get now, as an undergraduate, which would prepare me for a career in field archaeology?

Dr. Engelbrecht, who mentored so many of us, guided me through my education and early career until I was an experienced field archaeologist before even graduating with a Bachelor's. He even directed me to summer jobs where I could work as a field archaeologist; I was making money and gaining great experience in the field as a Junior and Senior.

Collectively, my education and experiences showed me that I selected a career path that I enjoyed and the particular specialties within anthropology (education and prehistoric archaeology) that best suited my interests and skill sets. Furthermore, my collective experience made it relatively easy for me to get accepted into multiple graduate schools and compete for jobs immediately after graduation. All this I gained mostly because I asked questions early on and followed through on advice and direction I was given. What would I have done if I dreaded my studies and experiences in field archaeology and tutoring? I would have gone back to the beginning and started all over again. I find most students change their majors multiple times as undergraduates. Why? Personally, I feel that colleges offer students their first chance at interacting with professionals in a wide range of fields. Think about it! On any given campus, you will find accomplished professionals in more fields than any high school student would imagine. Of course, the collective knowledge of these professionals won't just materialize in a student's mind. The student must ask questions and follow through on the advice a professor provides. The sooner a student does, the sooner he/she will find a suitable major and career path.

The Importance of Following Through on Advice Given

When I was advised to take specific classes or attend a conference, I followed through and did as advised. Such action was important for several reasons. First, those classes and experiences educated me on subject matter and career related opportunities. My ultimate foci in anthropology were decided largely based on what I learned through coursework and lectures I attended at conferences. For the record, as a person who has battled Obsessive-compulsive disorder my whole life, attending class let alone a conference was not an easy task, but I did it and was rewarded with knowledge.

A second reason why it's important to follow through on advice given is that such advisement often leads to great networking opportunities. I met many skilled and supportive colleagues through classes and conferences. These contacts later proved valuable as friends who helped me work out theories, connect with other anthropologists, and find work when I was unemployed. A few of the contacts I made even allowed me to work with them in the field, which provided me with further fieldwork experience as well as opportunities to co-author articles. Again, these experiences only aided my search for employment later on in addition to providing further knowledge of the field and research/job options.

The third reason it is important to follow through on advice given? When you leave college and apply for graduate school or a job, you will likely be asked to provide three to five letters of reference to attest to your personal and professional strengths. At the start of your career, these references will likely be mostly college professors you had as an undergraduate. When asking a professor to provide a letter of reference, you want that professor to be able to write that you were a dedicated and hardworking student. Yet, if you never followed through on advice, skipped classes, turned in assignments late or asked few questions, that professor will not be able to provide a good reference. Therefore, while in classes or seeking guidance from college faculty, follow through on advice as often as possible while also making sure you always strive to do your best. Otherwise, one good reference will be hard to find let alone three to five.

Chapter 7

Getting the Most out of Internships and Early Jobs

I've long been critical of the college model where a student completes one internship her/his Junior or Senior year, as if that is sufficient training to prep college students for the real world. In reality, a majority of college graduates have only one internship related to their career path by the time they graduate, which makes it hard to stand out from the ever-increasing pool of job applicants. To further complicate matters, many internships lack substance in that interns are often delegated to answering phones, sorting mail and filing client folders. While such experience is important, it hardly amounts to giving any intern a spectacular set of skills for use in the workforce. Do you see the pitfalls of the "one-internship" model?

My counter to the one-internship model, designed after my own experience as well as the experiences of many of my advisees, is to encourage students to track down career-relevant opportunities, beginning with the summer after their freshmen year, and to continually add experience up to and after graduation. This plan of action has skeptics, those complaining that "most fields offer no such opportunities for freshmen" or that "students will find it hard to get guidance towards relevant opportunities." Balderdash! Every major, every field, presents opportunities for freshmen or any novice to gain relevant experience with little prior experience or education. How do you track such opportunities down? As I've stated before, seek the guidance of the very professionals your college hired: the faculty. Think about it. Your professors, in most cases, have trained and mentored dozens if not hundreds of students before you even applied to the college. Make use of this experience as your professors have witnessed what worked and what didn't work for their advisees. Additionally, your professors were likewise freshmen at one time, too, which means they experienced defeat along with many successes. Why would you not take advantage of this wealth of information? Specifically, ask your professors the following, preferably during freshman year:

- What major/career-related experiences are options for freshmen?

- What class(es) will entry-level work in field require?

- What type of research/writing experience should freshmen seek to participate in (i.e. conducting surveys, writing articles for the school and/or local newspapers)?

- What internship-related experience should I look into in preparation for Junior and Senior year?

- What classes outside the major would provide great knowledge and experience for my career and my résumé?

Did you notice the redundancy from earlier sections? That's not by accident rather it's to reinforce the importance of asking questions as early as possible. That said, it's not just enough to obtain a job or an internship. What students need to also do is to obtain useful skillsets vital to their ultimate career success. What skillsets are essential for a student's respective field (i.e. organization, managerial experience, grant writing experience, etc.)? Again, this is a question to ask department professors. A common list would likely include:

- Able to work independently

- Computer-adept

- Creative

- Dependable

- Good listener

- Managerial experience

- Organized

With this list of skillsets in hand, approach every job as a means to attain the skills deemed important. What if a position obtained provides no obvious chance at managing/supervising others or computer-related responsibilities? Ask your employer for such opportunities. While there is no guarantee an employer will oblige such a request, I have found many employers appreciate such initiative and find ways to accommodate a creative employee. To gain experience relevant to the above skillsets, considering suggesting the following to an employer:

- Start/manage a Facebook and/or Twitter account for the company to help with marketing and community outreach (computer, leadership, organization, and marketing skills)

- Volunteer to organize a company-sponsored fundraiser (managerial, marketing, and money management skills)

- Arrange to assist in training new employees (leadership and managerial skills)

- Offer to organize storage space and order/manage company supplies (creativity and organizational skills)

All of these examples would reflect on an employee's initiative, creativity and dependability as long as he/she followed through on and provided the offered service. On a résumé or in a cover letter, a mention of these experiences would also help a job applicant shine. Of course, such experiences will have little weight if the job is not connected to a student's major/career goals. In fact, there will be times when a student will have no chance to obtain a paid position that is career-related. This is where volunteering can fill in the gaps in a student's/job seeker's experience.

Volunteering: Filling in the Experience Gaps

Unfortunately, there will be limits to gaining relevant experience, particularly at minimum wage-type jobs that many of us have as undergrads (I worked in a restaurant as a cook and dishwasher while an undergrad and graduate student, which paid bills but left no opportunity for archaeological or teaching experience). In such predicaments, how do you acquire the recommended skillsets? Volunteerism is the key to filling in such experience gaps. True, in most cases, volunteering pays nothing. However, gaining career-relevant knowledge AND having relevant experience to put on a résumé is a priceless accomplishment, which will significantly pay off in little time. How does it work? Again, interaction with professors and community professionals becomes key as a student must identify what experiences provide the best understanding of the career and résumé filler. After identifying relevant companies and positions to pursue, students must start reaching out to prospective businesses to inquire about volunteer opportunities. To aid students, it helps to track down businesses the college has established connections with through alumni or professors. With or without someone to make an introduction for a student, correspondence needs to occur where the student acknowledges her/his educational background and career interests. This is the student's chance to identify why a business could use the student. How is this done? First conduct research on a business with a focus on day to day operations, its five year plans, and any major initiatives underway. Then, through a formal letter or an email, contact a business representative and show how your talents and education fit the business's needs. In this correspondence, identify activities you'd like to contribute to, but make sure to indicate a willingness to help the business as is needed. Why? Volunteers willing to serve in a variety of capacities are a treasured commodity, and businesses will effort to make such volunteers happy by attending to the volunteer's requests as much as possible. How long should someone stay on as a volunteer? At a minimum, I suggest a year as that length of time will not only look good on a résumé (quantifiable experience), but it will also show dedication, both qualities a business will likely consider before elevating a volunteer to an employee. As a final note, if a student struggles to find opportunities, he/she should contact a local government official and inquire about volunteer needs of local businesses and not-for-profit organizations.

Relevant Volunteer Opportunities for Majors

Business Majors

- Accounting assistant for local public sports organization

- Marketing assistant for local radio or television show

- Office assistant for local business

- Public Relations or marketing aide for local small business

Communications/Journalism Majors

- Field assistant for reporter at local radio or television station

- Field investigator or interviewer for local newspaper or radio station

- Public Relations assistant for local radio or television station

- Writer and/or reporter for college newspaper or television station

Education Majors

- Aide for education staff at regional summer camps

- Aide for education programmer at local museum or library

- Tutor for local college or high school

Engineering Majors

- Aide for local plumber, mechanic or electrician

- Aide for construction foreman

- Maintenance assistant for local not-for-profit organizations

History Majors

- Aide for local genealogist

- Aide for local museum's education or collections departments

- Tutor for local college or high school

Math Majors

- Tutor for local college or high school

- SAT, MCAT or GRE tutor for local colleges or high schools

- Aide for local tax preparers or accountants

Natural Science Majors

- Tutor for local college or high school

- Aide for local laboratory or hospital

- Assistant for local zoo or natural history museum

- Aide at local animal rescue/rehabilitation facility

Social Science Majors

- Tutor for local college or high school

- Aide for local hospital staff

- Aide for local museum's collections department

Chapter 8

Tech-wise

I am ever-astounded by the fact that even with the ever-growing pool of technology available, most people, including adolescents, remain tech-inept. Sure, most people have smart-phones, tablets, laptops, and digital cameras, but relatively few are actually tech-savvy or, as I like to say, tech-wise. I routinely spend ample time showing students and staff how to navigate websites to track down information such as a business's contact information and staff listings. Likewise, I often teach college students and staff how to conduct detailed internet searches of people and events, which are actions that we 'techies' take for granted as being 'simple' procedures. With twenty years of experience in utilizing the internet and even more years invested in installing and operating computer programming, I can assure you that most people in the work force lack extensive skills in computer use and repair, which makes those of us with even a basic understanding of computers, programming and web usage a hot commodity for businesses.

What am I getting at? The more you know about computers, particularly the skill sets of programming, web searching, and repair, the greater your chances of gaining and *maintaining* employment. What skill sets in particular are important to acquire? The following is my list of essential computer abilities every student and job seeker should possess:

- Attain experience in website design programming.

- Create and/or manage a blog. Make certain to add routine updates, photographs and 'widgets' to enhance your blog and blogging skillset. Making the blog subject matter relevant to your career is a bonus.

- Familiarize yourself with platforms such as Twitter and their usefulness in reaching readers and potential customers.

- Gain experience in the use of Windows Word, Excel, PowerPoint and Publisher, which are four of the most utilized programs by businesses, government agencies and other entities.

- Work with a computer expert to learn how to add hardware to a computer such as a hard drive or a DVD drive.

Managing You Digital Footprint

Facebook, Twitter, Instagram and similar online platforms are a few keystrokes away for most inquisitive employers making it relatively easy to do a thorough and inexpensive background check on anyone. Why does this matter? Entities such as businesses and colleges want dependable, mature and professional students/employees in their respective folds, because having to hire and train people is expensive, both in money and time. So, right or wrong, businesses, colleges and a host of other entities will check a student's web footprint before admitting or hiring that student. To those hiring, a photo of an underage student drinking at a college party or involved in some sort of altercation gives the impression the student is immature to say the least. Consequently, it is important for everyone to strictly monitor what they post online. Think you're safe because you have tight controls on who can access your Facebook page? All it takes is for one of your friends to 'share' one of your less-than-appropriate posts to destroy your chances at getting a job. To that end, here is a list of things to consider in preparation for job hunting:

- Go through all your websites and remove inappropriate material. Ask friends to also delete any postings of you they have which are inappropriate (and link to you).

- Set up restrictions to limit who has access to your websites without your permission.

- Create online accounts (Facebook, Twitter, etc.) with unique usernames that only family and friends know. That will provide some additional privacy for you online.

- Conduct a Google search of yourself. In the event that you have inappropriate photos and/or postings that show up and you cannot remove them, make certain you create a flurry of new posts that are positive and continually build on those positive postings. Doing this may help bury posts and photos better left unseen.

- Don't post inappropriate material online, ever!

Chapter 9

Your First Job Search

Once a student has a degree completed, he/she will embark on the job search journey, a scary endeavor to say the least. Unfortunately, most students never receive instruction in conducting a job search and in handling the rejections that often come after applying for a position. To that end, I wanted to share a blueprint that I've found helpful for me, my students and my clients over the years. After being laid off the week before my wedding, I found this job search strategy provided a sense of calm and purpose while pursuing employment during a tough economy and in fields where traditionally few jobs surface even in good economic times (I was employed within three months after the layoff). While I am sure everyone's experience as a job seeker is unique, I know from my own experience as well as those of family, friends and students that progress during the job hunt is made easier when doing the following:

- **Keep a log of your search!** Write down the company applied to, the position applied for, and any contacts made at the company. Acknowledge if and when a cover letter and/or résumé were sent and what was the company's response. Keep copies of the paperwork sent as part of the application.

Figure 8

Company	Position	Date Applied	Material Sent	Contact	Response
ZXY	Field Supervisor	1/1/214	Résumé/Cover Letter	Jane Smith, VP of Marketing	Called for interview on 2/25/2014
					Interviewed/offered position on 2/28/2014
					Accepted Position on 3/1/2014
CBA	Field Supervisor	1/5/2014	Résumé/Cover Letter	Patrick Donnelly, CEO	Was informed my application was denied on 2/15/2014

You can find printable version from here: https://www.dropbox.com/s/zinscicssjjg0tl/ figure8.pdf?dl=0

- **Look for jobs in unique places!** For a start, job seekers should determine when their local newspaper updates and prints current job openings (often Sundays and Tuesdays). From there, promptly apply for any relevant positions. Additionally, job seekers should look at online job boards such as Monster.com, Indeed.com and Careerbuilder.com. Yet, these more traditional outlets miss a lot of job openings. Consequently, job seekers should expand their search to often overlooked job posting outlets such as company websites, town pennysavers, church bulletins, and social media platforms such as Facebook and Twitter where job seekers can relay their search to friends and family or connect directly with potential employers. Finally, job seekers should routinely check college websites for job openings. As many colleges and universities have become cities in and of themselves, these institutions need a growing diversity of employees beyond professors to include accountants, marketing and communication specialists, chefs, carpenters, mechanics, grant writers, counselors, nurses, financial advisors, archivists, architects, mechanical engineers, and electricians.

- **Send polished résumés and cover letters!** Any correspondence or materials submitted to a potential employer should be in a professional format and proofread by someone else. Preferably, résumés and cover letters should be written by individuals specialized in such writing formats. Fortunately, most colleges have Career Centers where students and Alumni can go to for résumé and cover letter assistance. Of course, résumé/cover letter samples can easily be found online. However, make certain samples selected pertain to the fields being applied to.

- **Contact employer using emails with professional usernames!** As a reminder, using emails with inappropriate/unprofessional usernames (i.e. Iamawesome@email.com, buttkicker@email.com, or crazyman101@email.com) will likely lead to an employer disregarding the applicant for any job. Recognize your email address as one of the first things about you an employer encounters so generate one that is clean and professional (i.e. firstname.lastname@email.com or lastname100@email.com).

- **Provide a phone number with an appropriate voicemail!** In the event an employer calls to set up an interview and the applicant is unavailable, an applicant's chances will diminish quickly if her/his voicemail is childish, comical or vulgar. A voicemail message will be viewed as an extension of the applicant so create a message that is professional and verifies whose phone the caller reached (i.e. "you've reached 555-555-5555. I am not available, but please leave a message and I will return your call as soon as possible."). For the record, voicemail messages that play music are a real turnoff to potential employers.

- **Don't harass a potential employer!** Once you apply for a job, be patient. Don't continuously call the employer asking where things stand with regards to your application. It's okay to call once to verify your application was received or to ask when decisions will likely be made. To call every other day to see what progress has been made may aggravate an employer and cause your application to be rejected.

- **Respond promptly to any correspondence!** When an employer contacts an applicant to request additional application materials or to set up an interview, respond immediately, preferably within twenty-four hours. Any delays on the applicant's part may likely convince the employer to move on to the next applicant.

- **Ask for feedback if you do not get an interview or the job!** This bit of advice is amongst the hardest to apply, but I am living proof it works. After being laid off and having applied for a few jobs I was not excited about, I came across a job I was uniquely qualified for. I applied, but I didn't even get an interview. I called and asked what made the difference for those applicants that received interviews and was informed those individuals submitted samples of academic enrichment workshops they created. A week later, after finding a similar position open at another college, I applied and included samples of academic enrichment activities I created in the past. I was interviewed and hired for the job within a month.

- **Be cordial!** My parents remain a guiding force for me, particularly with regards to how I interact with others. For Mom and Dad, politeness, understanding and forgiveness are essential virtues for everyone. I would argue that these virtues are particularly important during a job search. After my layoff, I was frustrated and scared. Newly married, I worried about how I would provide for my family. Yet, as frustrated as I got after receiving a rejection notice for a job I applied to, I held to the virtues my parents instilled in me. I sent thank you notes to employers for considering my application, even though my application was rejected. Why? First of all it's the right thing to do, because the employer did take time looking through my application materials. Secondly, being polite and showing gratitude is professional and may lead to your application being considered for other job openings at the employer, which is what happened to me on two occasions.

Overwhelmed? It's understandable if you are. Very little time is spent preparing undergraduates for job searching, which is a critical shortfall of higher education institutions. Yet, the more a new college graduate applies for work, the easier it will get. Just remember, when frustration sets in and it seems like you'll never find a job, it's important for you to reach out for support, which includes college professors and advisors, family and friends. Additionally, embarking on your first job search will be made easier if you include your alma mater's career center staff in the planning and implementation of your search. Career center staffs are one of the most underrated and underutilized resources at every college and university; don't forget to seek their assistance.

Chapter 10

Interviewing Skills

With twenty-plus years of experience career coaching, few things do I find to be as traumatic for job seekers as a job interview. Admittedly, I understand the angst that comes along with having to sit before an interviewer or hiring committee and sit their worrying as to what questions are going to be asked. I've been there myself more than a few times. However, there is an outlet for practicing for interviews long before an individual enters the *real* job market. That outlet is college.

As an undergraduate, students have multiple volunteer positions, jobs, grants and awards that they can apply for. In and of themselves, these opportunities offer wonderful opportunities for gaining great experience, which will better prepare students to excel in the job market. Even Work Study positions, often considered of little experiential value, provide valuable skill sets such as general computer programming and office assistant positions. Regardless, these opportunities usually entail a student being interviewed by one or more college personnel (faculty, staff and/or administrators). The anxiety and stress coexistent with such interviews, at least for college students, rivals interview-stress professionals experience when applying for jobs with small, medium and large companies. This is why students should look to such interviews as part of their college education, because these interviews can be just as valuable as any traditional course they take in college or graduate school.

Now, as I have stated before, a crucial step in preparation for much of my advice, including interviewing preparation, is to find a mentor to assist with preparations. I recommend the mentor be a professor from a major department related to a student's long-term career goals. Why? Professionals within each career field know what hiring committees and businesses are looking for in job candidates, specifically what skill sets are important for long-term success in a given field. This will be great information to have when going out into the world after graduation.

Interviewing Basics

Interviewing guides often unload a lot of typical advice, advice that many write off as myth or cliché.

Having participated as part of countless hiring committees, I can tell you that the *typical* advice is far from cliché and may often be the key to landing the job. To have true success and any chance of landing a position, here are the basic interview tips everyone must adhere to.

- **Show up early!** Be between fifteen to twenty minutes early, no more and no less. If you have never been to the business before, do a test run the week before so you know the route and where to park. Showing up late definitely will make the impression an individual is not serious or dependable. Showing up less than fifteen minutes early may delay things a bit should the interviewers require candidates to fill out any paperwork. As for showing up VERY early, that could make things awkward and uncomfortable for you and the hiring committee. What if another candidate for the job is being interviewed when you arrive? If you are super early, bring a book and read until fifteen to twenty minutes before the interview time.

- **Dress for success!** Advisement on what to wear to a job interview has remained pretty consistent over the last fifty years. Indeed, acceptable attire while on the job has evolved to more comfortable clothing, but the interview attire guidelines remain relatively unchanged. For men, a business suit, tie, dress shoes, and a dress shirt. For women, a pant suit or business dress is the best option. Navy blue is, in my opinion, still the most professional choice.

That said, other color schemes are gaining acceptance as far as interviews go. Just be cautious. Some may find a green, purple or orange color scheme daring and a sign of individualism. Others main find that same color scheme to be a sign of immaturity or a sign that the interviewee is not a team player.

- **Be cordial to the office support staff!** Do you want to know a secret? Hiring managers will often ask secretaries and interns what they thought of a candidate after said candidate leaves. Too often, job seekers treat support staff rudely either by responding curtly when asked to sign in or by ignoring the support staff altogether. Support staff is critical to the efficiency of a business, any business, and employers work hard to maintain a team environment. If a job candidate is rude to a secretary and word reaches the ear of the hiring manager, that candidate will unlikely get the job no matter how good her or his qualifications. So, always introduce yourself to the support staff present and send them a thank you note or email after leaving. That attentiveness and kindness will go a long way (if you are going to be coworkers, start off on the right foot). Additionally, and more importantly, it is the right thing to do.

- **Greet everyone on the hiring committee!** Before you take a seat, shake hands and introduce yourself to everyone on the hiring committee. Too often, interviewees greet the chair of a hiring committee and then simply nod to the others. Doing so could be disastrous for your chances of being offered the job. If you fail to acknowledge one of the hiring committee members, that snub will be what he/she remembers most. If possible, write down each committee member's name after sitting down (I'll explain why a little later). Also, bring enough copies of your updated résumé for everyone and offer it to the hiring committee members at the outset as some may not have a copy handy.

- **Use a firm handshake!** No, it is not a myth that a firm handshake can be the difference between getting a job and never having another chance at being considered for future openings at a company. Having served on multiple hiring committees, I am baffled by committee members overly fixated on a candidate's weak handshake. Don't leave open the door for such a close-minded view of your candidacy. Practice with friends until you have a firm handshake (though not so firm that you crush someone's hand).

- **Be prepared to listen and engage!** A job interview is a true test of an individual's observation abilities. Yet, being ever mindful of the words and actions of the hiring committee is only part of the game. The interviewee must take part in the conversation. True, you do not want to do most of the talking. However, you will be expected to answer and ask questions.

Remember, interviewees are not just applying for a position. Interviewees are also seeking to join a team, and the hiring committee wants to assess how that interviewee would coexist with the team. So, the interview is your time to show you can collaborate by adding to the flow of the discussion (i.e. listen and engage and answer and ask questions in ways that show your potential to connect to a company's needs and plans). I can't stress enough the importance of practice interviews to learn this skill set as quickly as possible. Doing research on the hiring committee and the department/company you are applying to will help you prepare for this.

- **Turn off your cell phone and do not look at your watch!** I think it's clear that if your cell phone goes off during an interview, you're not going to make a good impression. True, most people understand that little mistakes like that happen. Yet, it only takes one person on the hiring committee to be overly offended by a cell phone going off to irreparably damage an interviewee's chance of landing the job. As for your watch, looking at it repeatedly (or even once) could make the impression that you are not totally vested in the interview: not a good impression to make! Frankly, I think the best thing to do is to go into an interview with your cell phone off and your watch in a pocket.

- **Maintain good eye contact!** Whether you are interviewed by one person or ten, maintaining eye contact is a must. Look, interviewers know candidates are nervous. It probably wasn't that long ago that one or more of the interviewers sat in the same chair as the interviewee. Yet, hiring managers, staff and CEOs want people who can rise to the occasion and tackle tough situations. Maintaining eye contact shows fortitude, conviction and that the candidate is ready for a challenge. Additionally, for some interviewers, maintaining eye contact is a sign of respect. For such individuals, eye contact is often the first thing they comment about after the interviewee leaves. "The interviewee rarely looked at me" is a phrase I find often precedes a negative review of an interviewee after an interview. How do you maintain eye contact when interviewed by more than one person? Tricky, I know, but easier to do than you think. When entering an interview situation, determine who the lead person is (the person who will most directly be supervising the candidate hired). Once a question is asked, provide much of your eye contact to the person answering the question and the 'lead person'. To complicate things a bit, you also always have to periodically make eye contact with the others on the hiring committee. Doing practice interviews provides the best opportunity to practice this skill.

- **Be organized and prepared to take notes!** After sitting in on after over 100 interviews, you start to truly see what are the best (and worst) interview practices. For those interviewees who show up empty handed, basically with only their cell phone, the impression made is often that the interviewee is poor at preparing or he/she is arrogant and thinks the position is already hers/his. Neither is an impression you want to make. As for what this observation is based on? These are generally the two comments interviewers make after the interviewee leaves. When you go to an interview, bring a business portfolio with a legal pad inside and a couple pens and mechanical pencils to write with. Doing this portrays the interviewee as a 'professional' and as an individual eager to learn about the job and join the company. Now, as a past restaurant employee, some job interviews will not be as formal. However, even if applying for a dishwashing job, having paper and a pen to write with, should you need to write down any information, will be useful should the interviewer recommend other job openings or contacts the interviewee should look into. Being so equipped also shows, to many interviewers, that a job candidate is mature.

- **Don't look disheveled!** When I recommended that an interviewee bring a portfolio and a legal pad for writing notes, I am in no way suggesting that a job candidate should bring a desk's worth of equipment with her/him. When walking into an interview, it is imperative that you look organized and orderly, not sloppy and fidgety. What do I mean? Walk into an interview, greet all in attendance and then get settled into your seat as quick as possible. By having just a pad portfolio and pens and pencils (and extra copies of your résumé inside the portfolio), it is easy to just sit, open to the legal pad, pull out a pen, and be ready to engage with the interviewing committee. Any interviewee who takes time to rummage through a suitcase, satchel or other bag to get paper and a pen is likely going to appear unorganized to one or more of a hiring committee. Don't take the chance. Likewise, make certain your outfit or hair is not disheveled from the wind. When you arrive at the company, visit the restroom to make certain your hair and clothes are tidied up. Most of us interviewers are not overly concerned, but best prepare for those interviewers who nitpick about everything.

- **Bring a list of questions you may have.** Now, you may honestly have absolutely no questions about the job. Yet, interviewers often ask is the interviewee has questions. I recommend that you come up with some questions (three to five minimum) as to not ask questions may be perceived as a lack of preparation or interest in the job on your part (not a good impression to make). Once you have questions in mind, write them down on the legal pad you have in the portfolio; that way you won't forget. If you are uncertain of what questions to ask, here are a few standby questions to help you out:

- What are the company's five year goals?

- Is the company planning to expand operations in the near future?

- What are the biggest concerns of the company at this time?

- What are areas of collaboration that this position provides with regards to other departments?

- What computer programming/software changes are being planned for the near future? Will there be training provided through the company?

- What other areas of responsibility are you hoping to add to the position in the future?

- Does the company provide continuing education/training workshops onsite?

- What are the health and retirement benefits?

- What is the salary for the position?

- **Ask about salary and benefits.** Admittedly, asking for salary specifics, if not placed in the original job ad, is difficult. If the interviewer does not bring it up during the interview, the end of the interview is a good time to ask for salary and benefit specifics. What are the health insurance and retirement fund options? Is the salary negotiable based on experience?

In preparation for this discussion, it is imperative that you check out local job ads for similar positions to see what the salary range is. For those with little to no experience, taking a lower salary may be necessary as the experience gained will make it easier to negotiate a higher salary in the future. Your local unemployment office should have salary range information, and your college's career center may likewise have that information.

- **Reaffirm your interest in the position at the closing of the interview and ask what time table is for decisions.** When the interview is done, stand and shake each interviewer's hand and thank each for their time. Let them know that you are very interested in the job and the company's future outlook. It is now that an interviewee should also inquire as to what the next step is. Does the hiring committee need any additional information? Is there an estimate as to when interviewees will be updated as to their status (i.e. hired, put through to the next round of interviews, or not hired)?

- **Send thank you notes to the individuals that interviewed you.** A thank you note is the right thing to do for anyone who takes time to discuss things with you, whether it's about a job, a career path or anything else (I learned this from my Mom). In the event you forgot someone's name, you could either contact the hiring manager/hiring committee chairperson or you could simply write one to the chairperson thanking everyone (I strongly recommend that you send a separate note to everyone). Using note cards or writing a letter is the best option (I type up letters as my handwriting is too atrocious for note cards). At the very least, send an email written in a business letter format). For times when you can't remember the name of someone, visit the company's website, which may have staff listings with photos. Another way to find the information is to write to the hiring committee chairperson asking for every attendees office address. In doing so, the chairperson may provide you with all the hiring committee names without her/him ever knowing you forgot someone's name.

The Master Interviewer

The preceding tips, if followed, will go a long way to helping a job candidate stand out from the crowd of job applicants granted an interview. However, to truly shine during the interview stage, it is preparation for and responses to the following interview questions that often make the difference for the individual offered the job.

- **What do you know about our company?** Interviews often start off with this question, and believe me, you don't want to be in a position to say you really don't know much. Such a response could destroy your chances immediately. Now, it would be impossible to retain a thorough knowledge of the company and its employees, but you should be able to remember some major details and/or accomplishments of whom you are applying to. The following are questions you should know the answers to BEFORE you set foot in the interviewer's office in order to show you have done your research on the company: *How long has the company been in the area? What are the primary services/products provided by the business/institution? Who is the company's/institution's primary customer/client? What are major accomplishments of the business in the last two years? What are the company's short-term and long-term goals? What major grants or awards has the company recently received? What are major accomplishments of the company's staff in recent years? What are the company's major competition?* How do you find the answers to these questions? Check the internet and the company's website for 'latest news'.

- **What makes you the best candidate?** I am always nervous when someone responds to this question by simply saying "I'm the best person for the job; you don't need to interview anyone else." From my experience, people who say this have turned out to be horrible employees and colleagues who accomplish little other that talking endlessly about themselves. Consequently, if I am on an interviewing committee, don't say anything remotely like that. It comes off as arrogance and disrespectful as it suggests the job applicant is a harder worker than those on the hiring committee. Not a good impression to make. I suggest taking a different tact, because I believe every job applicant brings something different to the table. First, begin by stating "I am sure you are looking at a number of good applicants for the position." From there add that "given the listed job responsibilities, I feel I have a unique set of skills and experiences that will help me excel in the position immediately." From there, give examples to back up your claim. I suggest looking over the job description again, in preparation for this question, and connect your experiences and education to three to five of the major job responsibilities. It would be especially impressive if you could provide examples of where you took the initiative to develop programming, workshops or other unique services (for clients or colleagues). In the event you did create any workshops, programming or products, bring brief memos detailing your accomplishments. Including statistics of how you helped generate new business, increase client retention, exceed sales goals, or exceed company expectations would be a great addition.

- **What are your five year and ten year goals/plans?** In answering this question, I believe interviewees have the latitude to include unique goals they have: write a novel, travel overseas or run a marathon. That said, I think it is prudent for the interviewee to tie her/his goals to the company's goals, if known. Again, viewing the company's website or researching the company online through search engines should reveal such goals. Additionally, I advised interviewees to include a goal of seeking continued education via workshops or conferences, which can be attended and not require substantial time on the interviewee's part. You want to show a hiring committee you are not going to stop learning as they know they will need their employees to stay up to date on technology, ever-evolving industry standards, and market trends.

- **Why did you leave your last job or why are you looking to leave your current job?** This is often a tough question to answer as well as a question that is usually a cause for a hiring committee to reject an applicant. For those who were fired from their last job, I suggest you keep your answer simple. A possible answer is to say that the company was moving in a different direction and your position was no longer needed. If fired for poor performance, again keep your reply simple and straightforward: "My manager and I did not mesh well." I think it is always important to add a kind word about your current or former employers (i.e. "my boss was very passionate with her/his vision for the company's future"). If you verbally lash out about your old boss, the hiring manager or committee may wonder what you will say about them in the future. Yes, you could have the worst boss in history, but venting in an interview about that boss will not win you any points. If you quit your last job, again keep your response short and simple: "I didn't feel the position provided anymore room for growth while your company matches well with my abilities and goals."

- **Why are there employment gaps in your résumé?** For those who seem to have a new job every year, this will be tough to answer. Be up front if your positions were cut after a year due to economic crises faced by your employer and it took time to find new employment. If you took a medical or personal leave, and you were able to deal with the situation, make certain you let the interviewer(s) know that. I recommend that students/professionals try to complete three years at a job before moving on. Otherwise, the interviewer will likely be hesitant to hire the interviewee (it cost significant money and time to hire and train employees, which is why companies are hesitant to hire individuals who stay at jobs less than three years.

- **What will your references tells us about you?** Again, try and respond with answers that link up to the company's needs (in addition to comments that you are driven, a hard worker, dependable, timely and a great team player). For example, say that "my references would say that I would help you increase your customer base and rate of customer retention." Other good responses include:

- "My references would say that I would help in training other staff to become more comfortable with new technology."

- "My references would say that I am a great mentor for new employees."

- "My references would say that I am a great mediator for collaborations and dispute management."

- "My references would say that I am inquisitive and always monitoring new trends within the field."

- My references would say I am eager to collaborate with colleagues to improve company profile, offerings and achievements."

Final Interview Tips

In closing, the better prepared you are for the interview, the more likely you are to get hired. I recommend all college students and graduates speak with staff at their college's career center for preparation assistance. Many career centers will even provide mock interviews to help students practice; utilize such opportunities.

Finally, in this age of social media, it's imperative that your online footprint is as professional looking as possible. Many of us who check out a job applicant's online profile are understanding that teenagers post foolish things online (adults we are less understanding of). That said, many hiring managers are stringent in that they may hold a post of an applicant from when they were sixteen against them, even for something like skipping afternoon high school classes to attend a concert. Understandably, companies are especially vigilant in seeking out job applicants who post images of substance abuse, intoxication or bullying. You should not be doing any of these things. More to the point, you should not be posting such things as even the tightest security/blocking measures will not prevent a leak of inappropriate photos. All you need is for one of your friends to post a photo of you to ruin your chances of getting hired with a company. Take the time to erase inappropriate images, videos and posts from Facebook, Twitter and other social media sites BEFORE submitting a job application. While you are at it, be cautious as to what you 'Retweet', share or repost on social media as well. Potential employers could monitor that quite easily and would be less likely to hire someone who shares others' posts that are inappropriate or support one of the company's competitors.

Chapter 11

Concluding Remarks

Students receive a lot of feedback from teachers, guidance counselors, friends and family with regards to the rigors of college. As a result, students usually are mindful of the rigorous coursework and often fast-paced nature of campus living within a college setting. Unfortunately, very little time is spent preparing students about the career research and preparation they need to do in order to find the most suitable major while also preparing to compete for jobs immediately upon graduation. It is my hope that this book will rectify this common oversight.

With regards to your college career, I implore you to embrace the reality that this is your journey and no one else's. Pursue the major that fits your goals and desires. Think about it. Do you want to live someone else's dreams or do you want to pursue and live out your own dreams? Likewise, if you struggle with courses in your major, utilize all available support services your campus offers BEFORE abandoning the major and your dreams. I assure you that all majors include tough classes, which many students struggle with. Often, the students doing well in those courses are obtaining academic support from a professor or a tutor; there is no shame in asking for help. On the flipside of this argument, if after taking courses for general education requirements and conducting the aforementioned career research a student finds a new major and career goal to pursue, he/she should not feel obligated to stick with their initial major. You are permitted to change your mind! Now, if you decide your senior year that you'd like to pursue a new major, a change in major at that point may not be feasible (without spending more years as an undergraduate and thousands of dollars more in tuition). In such instances, the better decision may be to graduate and pursue a Master's in a different major. As for final advice with regards to getting the most out of your college years to prepare for career success, I leave the reader with this final list of advice to consider as these tips are important for all students regardless of major:

- **Find time to build up skill sets related to general office work.** Most professionals will work in, around or near an office setting at some point in their lives. Even business owners with no employees need to interact with a variety of outside agencies or individuals now and again, which is contact that will often involve an office setting. Knowledge of the mannerisms, organization, protocols and even basic equipment in general office settings will be of great benefit, even if it's just knowing that a secretary/office assistant can help cut through a lot of red tape (so treat these professionals nicely). I volunteered to watch the front desk at a computer lab at my alma mater, and that experience over three semesters provided a great glimpse at the inner workings of an office. The experience taught me a lot about how to network and how to better work in a team environment.

- **I've said it a lot, but it bears mentioning once more: LEARN Windows EXCEL!** Windows Excel is not nearly as difficult a program to learn as people think, and it provides an easy way to organize data for records, presentations and archiving. Furthermore, as most people are not proficient to any real extent, knowing Excel will provide an outlet for a professional to shine in front of bosses. There are a lot of online training programs (many free) to help anyone learn Excel and other Windows Office programming.

- **Remember that how you present yourself to others in a professional setting can have a profound impact on your success!** Everything from the way you dress for an interview to how you present yourself in writing (emails, résumés or otherwise) can matter with regards to getting a job or to landing a big promotion. As for your personal appearance as well as how organized you keep your office, it is better to be cautious: dress conservatively and maintain a clean, organized office. Appearances, especially early on, can make a profound and lasting impact on a person's career and success. As for writing, even established writers have their work proofread by others to avoid overlooking typos or more glaring mistakes in emails, letters and records. Don't make the mistake of thinking writing is not that important, because a lot of people out there are highly sensitive to writing mistakes.

- **Save textbooks from classes in your major!** Students will be amazed at how often terminology covered in classes become imperative to career success and promotion down the line. As humans are not computers, it becomes difficult to remember everything from our college days. That is why holding on to textbooks related to your major and/or career path is worth considering. Think of it this way. You spend $150 on a textbook and the college bookstore will pay you back $20 at the end of the semester for the book back. Foregoing the $20 and holding onto a text, meanwhile, provides a great reference book for the future. Yes, textbooks are usually out of date by the time they hit store shelves. However, the bulk of definitions, particularly regarding theories, remain intact for decades after publication. Hold on to the textbooks from you major – trust me.

- **Save charts, graphs or other visuals provided in classes that helped clarify a topic or term!** Remember those pesky theories and methodologies covered in college courses? Of course you don't, at least not all of them. PowerPoint slides, handouts and other class documents can be of big help later on in your career just as is the aforementioned case of course textbooks as such illustration-heavy resources help breakdown even the most complex of terms. When shredding or otherwise disposing of study aids from your college years after graduation, think twice about discarding major/career-related materials as they may prove helpful for future meetings, programming or career changes.

- **Leave college with a list of books that professors from your major believe to be 'classics' (or forward-thinking in their premise) and make certain you read them.** Many students forego graduate school relying on a bachelor's or an associate's degree as their 'terminal' degree. For many career paths, that is totally acceptable. However, a lot of material covered in graduate school could hold relevance with regards to career success. Information taught in graduate school could provide unique skill sets, which could help an individual excel in the field. At a more basic level, knowledge of books, theories and methodologies discussed in graduate school may become a focal point in a job interview. Not attending graduate school is not an excuse for not knowing said material. Therefore, prior to leaving college, ask your major advisor for a list of books, theories and professionals he/she recommends you know about, and then treat that list as a final homework assignment.

- **Continue your education even into retirement!** The world is not static, and neither should be your education. Keeping up on world events alone is crucial for anyone to be an informed voter and professional. Knowledge of new developments within a career allows a professional to remain a contributor to a company's present and future, which means greater job security. Being current on industry developments also means an individual has greater value should he/she seek a new job. Additionally, most peoples' career interests change over time, which translates to a need to study up on any new interests. Professionals within your field can likely guide you to 'continuing education' outlets, many of which will be connected with professional organizations. An added benefit to continuing your education is that you will likely be more aware of coming industry changes/developments, which will allow you to adapt quicker to such developments.

- **In keeping with *continued education*, keep up on technological advances, particularly advances within your field.** Technology changes in all fields, and much of the technological changes are of use in most if not all fields. Those who stay up to date will be better able to adapt to future field developments. Those who don't will find it difficult to be competitive and find long-term employment. As for where to learn new technology? Local school districts often provide technology classes that are inexpensive ($10-$25) and held at night or on weekends. Likewise, there are multiple outlets online to learn technology. Please also keep in mind that often, businesses will pay for their employees to take continuing education classes as they want to stay ahead of the competition with regards to technological developments. See if your employer will pay for technological training. As a personal recommendation, I advise everyone to learn about social media outlets like Twitter, Facebook, and blogs. More and more companies are recognizing the importance of these outlets for reaching current and new customers. So, those of us proficient in these technologies will have a decided advantage when applying for promotions or new jobs.

Now for readers thinking I am advocating that college is all work and no play, nothing can be further from the truth. Joining clubs or sports teams and hanging out with friends is important for stress relief, personal growth, and a fulfilling life. In fact, there are a number of suggestions I give my advisees that

I think all college students should consider alongside their studies including:

- **Find time to read a book everyday even if it's only for twenty minutes.** My parents read endlessly, which served as an example my siblings and I live by. Reading helps distract us from stress in our lives, which is important for health and longevity. Reading also helps us expand our imagination, and that benefit could ultimately help individuals be more creative at work. From my experience, creative people make a greater impact in the world and in their own lives.

- **Utilize the gym and pool facilities at your college and go there with your close friends for a good workout as well as good down-time.** When I was an undergraduate, we were required to take 2.0 credits worth of physical education classes, which forced us to utilize the campus gym facilities. I wish this was still a part of degree requirements, because I learned a great deal about the human body's needs as well as what forms of exercise I liked best. Most campuses have a range of facilities that include pools, tracks, ice rinks, and basketball courts. As you are paying for these services through student activity fees, USE THEM! When you do, you will find a great outlet for releasing stress, becoming more fit, and connecting with new friends. Give it a chance!

- **Visit several of the cultural institutions within the immediate vicinity of your college including history, science and art museums.** After being told what is 'art' and what is 'important history', our college years offer a chance to truly explore art and history and determine for ourselves what we think is important and significant. I encourage every student to walk through an art gallery and see what art forms peak their interests. Furthermore, explore a history museum or historical society and give history a new opportunity to thrill you. Doing this, outside of any class requirements, may lead you to new experiences and the realization that you've missed out on a lot of humanity's glorious past.

- **Attend one play or musical on campus during your undergraduate years. Even better, join the cast or crew for one production.** The performance arts are a true gift, often making televisions and the internet appear mundane. The experience of sitting in a theatre and hearing and watching a performance live can provide an experience beyond all imagining. Whether it's a comedic musical, a dramatic play, or a symphony's performance of Mozart's greatest works, this could be one of the most memorable experiences of your life.

- **Attend at least one field trip with your department classmates.** As you become an upperclassman, you will begin to interact a lot more with those in your major. I encourage you to attend a department field trip if given the chance as this will help increase the bond between you. In the immediate sense, these department-mates can commiserate with you over tough classes and experiences while like-wise offering a readymade study support for classes and senior projects/theses. Later in life, these connections may form the basis for a solid network capable of helping you find jobs or even colleagues with which to conduct a groundbreaking study or start a fortune 500 company. I can't stress enough though just how great it is to have a small group of friends to vent with, friends that know the hell you are going through in one or more classes.

- **Attend a couple sporting events such as a soccer, football or basketball game.** Sporting events can be a great stress relief during any time of an academic year. Think about a stressful time in your life and the frustration you felt. Wouldn't you have loved an opportunity to scream out loud to release that frustration? Yes, sporting events can be a great way to network, connect better with friends, and increase your bond with your alma mater. For me, it's always great to attend a sporting event just for the thrill of screaming out loud to vent while opposing teams beat the hell out of each other. What can I say? Football and hockey are big in Buffalo, New York.

These recommendations are geared towards having fun while planning and preparing for your future. Who knows, such experiences may help you find your career path. With all said and recommended, I congratulate readers on their efforts to gain an education and pursue their dreams. You now know what you need to do. Go do it! Take care!

Appendix 1: My Career Preparation and Research Checklist

Freshman Year:

____ Completed Career Assessment at college's Career Center.

____ Went over Career Assessment results with Career Center Staff Member.

____ Discussed Majors of interest with Department Faculty (potential job opportunities, career paths and courses in other majors to consider taking).

____ Discussed with Faculty jobs and volunteer opportunities available to undergraduates, which would provide good experience.

_____ Discussed the need/usefulness of studying abroad to career goal with Department Faculty.

_____ Completed introductory classes in Major.

Sophomore Year:

_____ Selected concentration within Major and Department Advisor.

_____ Discussed graduate school needs and options for Major/career goals with Department Advisor and/or Department Faculty.

_____ Started taking appropriate non-Major courses that would complement career goals.

_____ Connected with off-campus professionals (particularly Alumni) to further Investigate job options related to Major as well as useful coursework to consider taking in preparation for the student's career goals.

_____ Attended campus lectures, guest speaker events and other Major-related events.

_____ Discussed with Department Faculty current career goals and related long-term educational needs. Started looking into required graduate exams and took 'practice' exams when offered.

Junior Year:

_____ Completed internship(s); sought additional career/Major guidance from internship Supervisor.

_____ Began studying for and took graduate school exams (GRE, GMAT, LSAT, MCAT, etc.).

_____ Started attending off-campus conferences related to Major and career interests.

Senior Year:

_____ Completed additional internship(s); strengthened contacts with community leaders, not-for-profit institutions and businesses related to student's Major/career path.

_____ Completed graduate school exams (GRE, GMAT, LSAT, MCAT, etc.).

_____ Compiled list of references from professors; obtained three to five written recommendations from amongst these references.

_____ Through college Alumni Office, connected with Alumni from Major to investigate career options as well as local and national job openings. Also investigated all benefits Alumni Office offers to graduates.

_____ Worked with Department Faculty and Career Center staff to construct an updated résumé and individualized cover letters for each job student applies to.

_____ Obtained a copy of college transcript after graduation to insure information is accurate.

Appendix 2: Résumé Writing 101

A solid, professional-looking résumé is crucial for most job seekers in their attempts to get an interview. What are the essentials of a good résumé? You will find a variety of opinions on this matter. As a recent graduate, it's understandable that any résumé you have will be limited in regards to experience (in most cases). As a professional résumé writer, I like to keep résumés simple, straightforward and one page in length, because when I am on a hiring committee reading a hundred résumés, I like to be able to quickly locate the data relevant to the job opening. So, to keep things simple, the following is a list of recommendations for your résumé.

- **Provide accurate contact information.** You would be amazed at how often résumés contain old addresses or cell phone numbers. At the top of any résumé should be a street address, apartment number and the best phone number with which a hiring manager can contact you.

- **List your education including degrees and certifications.** Recent graduates often don't have advanced certifications, but any certification relevant to your career path should be included. As many jobs now require a college degree just to be considered, I usually advise job seekers to put the education section immediately after their name and contact information.

- **Include a 'Summary of Qualifications' section.** In this section, list your primary strengths attained through education and experience. This can include certifications (CPR, résumé writer, book keeping, insurance estimator, carpentry, etc.). Listing any computer programming experience is an option for here as well. What is most important is to list qualifications relevant to the job you are applying for.

- **List experience in reverse chronological order.** List each job you had/have and include a brief listing of responsibilities you had at each job. It is important to list those job duties relevant to the job you are applying for. Additionally, you should include any accomplishments you attained at each job such as awards received or initiatives you led/orchestrated.

- **List computer proficiencies.** Most jobs now require employees to manage databases or programming related to processing orders and payments. Consequently, it often helps to list what programs an individual has mastered. Such programming includes Excel, Access, PowerPoint, Word and any number of programs that are industry specific. Check with professors to see what programs employers are looking for and learn those programs. If your résumé is bursting at the seams and already one page after the aforementioned sections, it is permissible to put computer proficiencies in the 'Summary of Qualifications' section.

- **List of Professional Affiliations.** As a recent graduate, most jobs will not be too picky about a student's membership in industry-relevant organizations. However, if you're lacking in experience (professional and/or volunteer), adding a few professional memberships to your profile can be helpful in making you a standout. What's more, such organizations often provide members with free continuing education classes and job listings.

- **Should I include a 'Job Objective'?** Most of us who write résumés often do not include a job objective. Why? Frankly, these 'objectives' use up valuable space on a one page résumé, which we feel is better served listing experience and viable skill sets relevant to the job being applied for. Having served on multiple hiring committees, I find most of us find that the job objectives on résumés are vague and thereby meaningless. If a new graduate has limited experience, and needs something to fill up the one page of her/his résumé, a job objective could serve well here. However, make the objective relevant to the specific job being applied for. The following résumés provide examples of all this advice in action. The job objective, if used, would appear after the name and contact information.

100 HOME STREET • SOMEWHERE, NY 00000
555.555.5555 • USERNAME@EMAIL.COM

JANE SMITH

EDUCATION

2014	Buffalo College of Law	Buffalo, NY

Associates, Paralegal Studies

SUMMARY OF QULAIFICATIONS

- Proficiency in securing evidence for litigation including digital records, phone logs, employment files and business contracts.
- An aptitude for quickly identifying relevant state and federal court decisions   relevant to cases.
- Expertise in prepping legal team for arguments and case histories of potential use by opposing counsel.
- Adept in use of Excel and the use of multiple legal coding/billing software.

PROFESSIONAL EXPERIENCE

2011-Present	Burns Law Firm	Buffalo, NY

Senior Legal Researcher, Business Litigation Unit
- Coordinated research of legal histories and precedence in areas Contract, Insurance and Trademark Law.
- Developed Excel-based database for compilation of trial histories to provide quicker access to future researchers of past legal proceedings.
- Served as liaison for partners to obtain and submit legal documents and offers from opposing counsel.

2010-2011	Burns Law Firm	Buffalo, NY

Senior Legal Researcher, Business Litigation Unit
- Coordinated evidence cataloging and completed court requests for evidence and depositions.
- Assisted in research of historical proceedings to aid in providing precedence to support legal teams' court actions.
- Developed Excel-based database to store digitized copies of updated versions of legal, billing and research departments' forms.

PROFESSIONAL AFFILIATIONS

America Bar Association
Western New York Bar Association

You can find printable version from here:
https://www.dropbox.com/s/gao0nj71jcoev95/
figure9.pdf?dl=0

100 HOME STREET • SOMEWHERE, NY 00000
555.555.5555 • USERNAME@EMAIL.COM

JANE SMITH

JOB OBJECTIVE

To serve as a paralegal at the Miranda Doe Law Firm, utilizing my skills in legal research, Business Law and trial proceedings to aid the firm and its clients.

EDUCATION

| 2014 | Buffalo College of Law | Buffalo, NY |

Associates, Paralegal Studies

SUMMARY OF QULAIFICATIONS

- Proficiency in securing evidence for litigation including digital records, phone logs, employment files and business contracts.
- An aptitude for quickly identifying relevant state and federal court decisions   relevant to cases.
- Expertise in prepping legal team for arguments and case histories of potential use by opposing counsel.
- Adept in use of Excel and the use of multiple legal coding/billing software.

PROFESSIONAL EXPERIENCE

| 2011-Present | Burns Law Firm | Buffalo, NY |

Senior Legal Researcher, Business Litigation Unit
- Coordinated research of legal histories and precedence in areas Contract, Insurance and Trademark Law.
- Developed Excel-based database for compilation of trial histories to provide quicker access to future researchers of past legal proceedings.
- Served as liaison for partners to obtain and submit legal documents and offers from opposing counsel.

| 2010-2011 | Burns Law Firm | Buffalo, NY |

Senior Legal Researcher, Business Litigation Unit
- Coordinated evidence cataloging and completed court requests for evidence and depositions.
- Assisted in research of historical proceedings to aid in providing precedence to support legal teams' court actions.
- Developed Excel-based database to store digitized copies of updated versions of legal, billing and research departments' forms.

You can find printable version from here:
https://www.dropbox.com/s/whbvqo92lprlenp/
figure10.pdf?dl=0

Appendix 3: Cover Letter Writing 101

Like the résumé, a cover letter is a critical element for job seekers, often providing a hiring manager or committee with their first glimpse at a candidate. Now, where a general résumé may suffice for multiple jobs you apply to, cover letters should be reworked for every job applied to. Why? You want a hiring manager to think you are truly interested in the position you are applying to verses just sending out résumés in the hope of finding any job until you land THE job. Companies often spend thousands on job searches only to have the applicant chosen leave the company six months later for another job. These common occurrences then leave companies thousands of dollars in the hole only to have to spend thousands more for another applicant search. Hiring managers can easily spot generic cover letters and will often disregard such applicants assuming they are not looking to stay at the company long term. When hiring managers find a personalized letter, however, they are more likely to take the applicant seriously. To that end, here are things to include in a cover letter as well as a sample of an impactful cover letter.

- **Use the heading from your résumé.** Consistency in formats and styles between résumés and cover letters shows professionalism. To have a résumé in one style (heading, spacing, font, etc.) and the cover letter formatted entirely different is sloppy and makes for a poor impression.

- **Use a formal business letter format.** You should put the date after your heading followed by the name and full contact information of the person you are sending the cover letter to. In the event you don't have a specific name to address the letter to, write to the 'Hiring Manager'. What is an even better choice in such circumstances is to call the company and ask if there is a specific person you should address the letter to.

- **Open the letter indicating you have relevant experience and reference the job being applied for.** Let's say your application is received at a time the company is hiring for multiple positions, and your application gets placed in the wrong file. How will they know what job you are applying to? Sure, they can probably figure things out somewhat quickly, but do you want to leave them guessing? Is that the first impression you want to make? Additionally, as hiring managers will likely be looking at over 100 applications, using the first sentence to clearly state you have the required experience will likely get your application due consideration.

- **Indicate your skill sets relevant to the position.** Using cues from the 'Summary of Qualifications' section of your résumé, list in a bulleted format a few key skill sets that will make you a standout for the position. Why the bulleted format? It makes for easier reading, which is what hiring managers prefer when faced with 100 cover letters.

- **Include a brief paragraph on relevant experience.** Like a résumé for a recent graduate, a cover letter should be no more than one page in length. Consequently, while detailing work experience relevant to the sought position is important, it needs to be concise. Try and keep this section to 100 words.

- **Close the letter by thanking the hiring manager for her/his time.** It is important to show professional courtesy with any business correspondence as a hiring manager will consider how you will treat the staff and clients of the company you are applying to. Also, it's the right thing to do. Additionally, this final paragraph should include your indicating a wish to speak with the hiring manager to further discuss your skills. You may also wish to say that you will call in a specified time frame to discuss your application, but that may be risky as some hiring managers may feel such statements as pushy.

- **Sign letter and type your name under your signature.** If you only sign a letter and your signature is unreadable, it might prove frustrating for the hiring manager to figure out who you are. For safety's sake, type your name after the signature.

JANE SMITH

October 20, 2015

Miranda Doe
Senior Partner
Miranda Doe Law Firm
101 Main Street
Somewhere, NY 00000

Dear Ms. Doe:

I am an accomplished paralegal with five years experience assisting attorneys with trial and settlement preparation within the areas of civil and criminal litigation, with particular specialization in business law. I would like to bring my collective experience and success to the paralegal position you are currently advertising, specifically contributing the following to the Miranda Doe Law Firm:

- Proficiency in securing evidence for litigation including digital records, phone logs, employment files and business contracts.
- An aptitude for quickly identifying relevant state and federal court decisions relevant to cases.
- Expertise in prepping legal team for arguments and case histories of potential use by opposing counsel.

After completing an Associate's in Paralegal Studies, I joined the Burns Law Firm in Buffalo where I assisted firm partners with legal research. Having excelled in coursework in Business and Contract Law, I was assigned to the firm's Business Litigation Unit where I coordinated evidence cataloging and completed court requests for evidence and depositions. After my first year, I was promoted to senior legal researcher and tasked with researching and summarizing legal precedence in preparation for trials. Collectively, I believe my experience and education will enable me to assist your team and clients in preparing for any legal action, an opportunity I enthusiastically welcome.

I would appreciate an opportunity to meet to further discuss my paralegal, litigation and research experience at your earliest convenience. I may be reached at (555) 555-5555 or via email at username@email.com. Thank you for your time and consideration.

Sincerely,

Jane Smith
Jane Smith

You can find printable version from here:
https://www.dropbox.com/s/xh4x2b5uzxu7530/
figure11.pdf?dl=0

Dear reader,

We hope you enjoyed reading *The Career-Minded Student*. Please take a moment to leave a review, even if it's a short one. Your opinion is important to us.

Discover more books by Neil O'Donnell at https://www.nextchapter.pub/authors/neil-odonnell

Want to know when one of our books is free or discounted? Join the newsletter at http://eepurl.com/bqqB3H

Best regards,
Neil O'Donnell and the Next Chapter Team

The Career-Minded Student
ISBN: 978-4-86751-598-3 (Mass Market)

Published by
Next Chapter
1-60-20 Minami-Otsuka
170-0005 Toshima-Ku, Tokyo
+818035793528
22th July 2021

www.ingramcontent.com/pod-product-compliance
Lightning Source LLC
LaVergne TN
LVHW031238190726

843491LV00012B/3044